FOUR
SISTERS

FOUR SISTERS

THE HISTORY OF

RINGSEND, IRISHTOWN, SANDYMOUNT AND MERRION

KURT KULLMANN

The
History
Press

Leabharlanna Poibli Chathair Baile Átha Cliath
Dublin City Public Libraries

For three brothers

John Carl, Michael Denis, Christopher Hans

When you grew up you stayed sons
but you also became friends.
Thank you.

First published 2017

The History Press Ireland
50 City Quay
Dublin 2
Ireland
www.thehistorypress.ie

The History Press Ireland is a member of Publishing Ireland,
the Irish book publishers' association.

British Library Cataloguing in Publication Data.
A catalogue record for this book is available from the British Library.

ISBN 978 0 7509 8435 5

Typesetting and origination by The History Press

Printed and bound by TJ International

CONTENTS

INTRODUCTION

COASTLINE

Dublin Bay keeps changing. The changes to its western end during the last millennium around the mouths of the rivers Liffey, Tolka and Dodder were quite far-reaching and many of those changes were caused by humans. It is not possible to trace all changes in detail, as old maps are less exact than modern ones. Sometimes clues to a former borderline between land and sea are found when laying foundations for new buildings. The map of a probable shape of the Liffey mouth at the time of the Battle of Clontarf shows a remarkable difference to the situation today.

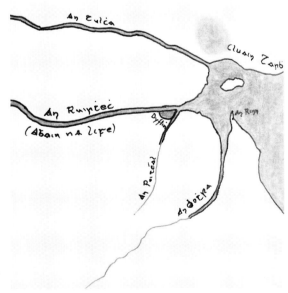

Western end of Dublin Bay, the Battle of Clontarf.

The four villages (suburbs) of Dublin 4: Ringsend, Irishtown, Sandymount and Merrion are often referred to as the four sisters, having many things in common, but also some very individual characteristics. Most parts of the four villages are built on low-lying land, much of which has been reclaimed from the sea. Sandymount DART Station is only 2.5m above sea level (Malin Head Ordnance Datum). Much of the land in these coastal villages lies even lower, some of it below sea level. The whole area is partly sandy, partly swampy or marshy and was often inundated for many centuries. Former landlords – the Fifth, Sixth and Seventh Viscounts Fitzwilliam of Merrion and Barons Fitzwilliam of Thorncastle – had clay dug from the southern part of this area to make bricks when they developed Merrion Square, Fitzwilliam Square and the area between them in the eighteenth century. This activity lowered the ground level even more and Richard, Seventh Viscount Fitzwilliam, had to build a wall at the edge of the sea to protect his land. This wall still exists and has protected Merrion and Sandymount for more than 200 years from being submerged by the sea, though lately insurance companies have insisted that it is not quite high enough.

As far as distance from Dublin city centre is concerned, Lewis[1] mentions that Ringsend is 1½ miles (2.5km) from the General Post Office, Sandymount 2 miles (3.5km) and Merrion 3 miles (4.8km). Lewis includes Irishtown in his Ringsend entry. Modern maps give a distance of 1⅞ miles (3km) from the GPO to Irishtown.

TOWNLANDS AND VILLAGES

In Ireland townlands are the smallest administrative divisions of land. They are also the oldest divisions as they arose in Gaelic culture and go back to times before the Norman invasion. Pembroke Township had fifteen townlands. Present-day Dublin 4 added two whole townlands and parts of two more. This enlargement was caused by the expansion of Donnybrook village southwards into the former barony of Rathdown. Baronies were subdivisions of counties from the time of the Tudors until the Local Government (Ireland) Act 1898.

Pembroke Township did not exceed the borders of the former barony of Dublin. The fifteen (or nineteen) townlands grew into six villages – or seven if Baggotrath is counted as a village in its own right. The four coastal villages spread out from the original townlands of the same name. Over the years some of them increased their area considerably. Two sketches show the differences in the example of Ringsend. In those maps the borders of the

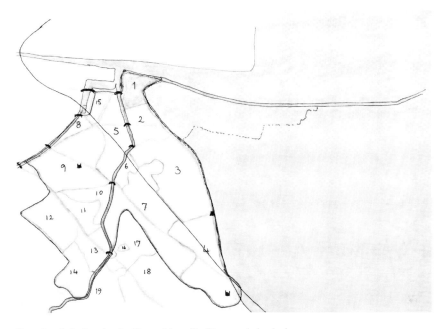

Townlands in Pembroke Township with Ringsend shaded.

1=Ringsend	6=Ballsbridge	11=Fortyacres	16=Annefield
2=Irishtown	7=Smotscourt	12=Donnybrook West	17=Simmonscourt
3=Sandymount	8=Baggotrath North	13=Donnybrook East	18=Priesthouse
4= Merrion	9=Baggotrath East	14=Clonskeagh	19= Roebuck
5=Beggarsbusch	10=Baggotrath	15=South Lotts	

townlands or villages are shown with the border of Pembroke Township in a stronger line. Major roads and the railway are also shown.

The map shows that the townland 'Ringsend' is situated east of the Dodder with the Liffey as border to the north, the sea to the east and what now is Oliver Plunkett Avenue as border to Irishtown in the south.

The map of the villages of Pembroke Township shows that the village 'Ringsend' includes nearly the whole of the townland South Lotts (onto the railway) and the northern part of townland Beggarsbush (up to and including Shelbourne Park Stadium and Shelbourne Park Apartments).

In the case of Irishtown the difference is even greater as the village does not only include the part of Beggarsbush townland south of Ringsend but also most of the Poolbeg Peninsula that was reclaimed from the sea south of the South Wall.

It has to be said here that those village borders are not universally accepted. The borders as shown on the map sketched above are suggestions rather than

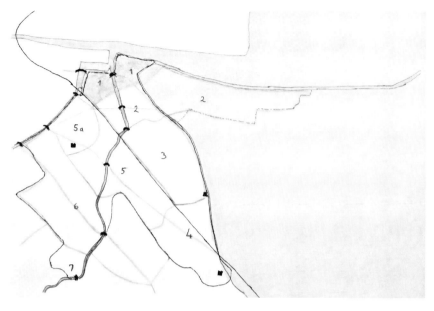

Villages in Pembroke Township, again with Ringsend shaded.

1 = Ringsend	3 = Sandymount	5 = Ballsbridge	6 = Donnybrook
2 = Irishtown	4 = Merrion	5a = Baggotrath	7 = Clonskeagh

exact borders. It seems more convenient to take the railway as a border to the west instead of sticking to old townland borders, which were more often than not determined by property rights. South of Sandymount Avenue this adjustment has been made by the OS map of 1907, compared with the map of 1837. Holyrood Castle, however, and its surroundings east of the railway are in Smotscourt townland, which in its bulk has turned into the southern part of Ballsbridge. Now the part east of the railway is regarded by most people as part of Sandymount village. The Roman Catholic Parish Church of Sandymount, the Church of Our Lady Star of the Sea, is on Irishtown townland and 'Sandymount' Martello Tower at the other end of Sandymount is in Merrion townland, but most people would think of them as part of Sandymount.

GEOGRAPHY OR HISTORY?

The most common way to list the four coastal villages of Dublin 4 is in the geographical sequence from north to south: Ringsend, Irishtown,

Sandymount and Merrion. This is, however, not the sequence in which the villages developed. Seen historically, Merrion is the eldest, most likely starting in the late thirteenth or early fourteenth century, followed by Irishtown which became established in the fifteenth century. After Irishtown follows Ringsend which according to some authors might be older, but most regard it as developing into a village in the late sixteenth century. The youngest is Sandymount, which only began to develop in the last quarter of the eighteenth century. Even though sisters are usually listed according to age, here the geographical line is followed, as if taking a walk from the Poolbeg lighthouse along the coast to the southern border of Dublin city. Despite the fact that in modern times Irishtown quite often is described as if it were incorporated into Ringsend, and Merrion as if it were part of Sandymount, here each village will be mentioned as a separate and complete unity, each with its own character and history.

EARLY HISTORY OF THE AREA

PRE-NORMAN TIME

Latest research indicates that the first humans reached Ireland in the Palaeolithic Era, around 12,000 years ago. The area south of Dublin, however, seems to have been populated much later. The first signs of people living there date from the end of the Mesolithic times, *c.* 4,000 BC, with finds on the north shore of the mouth of the Liffey and on Dalkey Island.

After that there was a long gap. Not that there were no people around – there might have been – but nobody knows anything about them. That people were living at that part of the coast is in no doubt, but it has been documented only much later.

The first event in this area for which a definite and documented date exists was the arrival of St Palladius on the Dublin and Wicklow coast in AD 431, sent by the Pope to the Christian inhabitants of Ireland as their first bishop. That of course means that at this early time it was already known in Rome that there were Christians in Ireland. As those Irish Christians possibly were slaves who had been captured in Wales, England or France, St Palladius's arrival was not welcomed by the slave owners who did not want their slaves, who were their property, meddled with by some weird stranger. St Palladius is said to have built a few churches, but then he himself evaded the opposition and went to Scotland to Christianise the Picts. He had asked some of his companions to stay, however, even leaving them some books, which in those days were very valuable possessions.

Before the arrival of the Vikings (also called Norse, Ostmen and sometimes Danes, though the latter did not include all of them) the coast south of the Liffey was part of Cualand (also Cualann or Cuala), settled by the Uí Briúin Cualand.

The Uí Briúin appear to have occupied the coastal district south of the River Liffey at a very early date, perhaps before AD 500, and to have gradually extended their territory further to the south.[1]

The Uí Briúin Cualand were part of the Uí Dúnchada and in the twelfth century the ruling family of the Uí Dúnchada were the Mac Gilla Mo-Cholmóc who accepted the Normans as overlords later and changed their name into FitzDermot after one of their chiefs, Diarmaid Mac Gilla Mo-Cholmóc.

The Dublin area suffered Viking attacks from the eighth century on, but most of those early attacks were short raids, looking for treasure and for people that could be sold as slaves. In the ninth century the Vikings established a permanent post on a rise between the Liffey and Poddle rivers. This grew into a town of probably a few hundred people, and the surrounding area became a kingdom, which the Vikings called Dyfflinarskiri. From its beginning until the Normans arrived in Leinster and defeated the Norse, their distant cousins, the south-east coast of Dublin Bay belonged to this kingdom. Through a grant of Richard de Clare, in Ireland better known as Strongbow, to his companion Walter de Ridelesford, it is known that the Mac Torcaill family, the last dynasty of the Norse kingdom of Dublin, held land in this coastal area. Even after the beheading of the last Norse king Ascall Mac Torcaill (also referred to as Askulv Mac Thorkil or in Norse as Höskellr Thorkelson) some members of this family held land in what now is south County Dublin and north County Wicklow.

AGE OF THE COASTAL VILLAGES

The majority of historians regard Merrion as the oldest of the four villages, as it grew around Merrion Castle, which was first mentioned in 1334 but probably was built during the thirteenth century. This castle was situated where St Mary's Asylum for the Female Blind used to be, which now is St Mary's Centre of the Religious Sisters of Charity. T.W. Freeman held another opinion about the age of these villages. According to John W. de Courcy[2] Freeman thought that Ringsend was older than Merrion and started at the same time as Dublin. These were two different settlements that occupied two patches of slightly raised and therefore dry ground.

As far as Irishtown is concerned, John W. de Courcy says:

Human habitation at Ringsend (An Rinn) dates back almost certainly before 900. So far as this book is concerned, it has always been there. It seems likely that the area of Irishtown was inhabited at the same time, that the two were one community.

Most historic publications describe the coastal villages as younger. Thorncastle (roughly at modern Williamstown) and Merrion were fortified mansions to guard the Pale. They were probably built in the thirteenth century. Irishtown as a village is mentioned in the fifteenth and Ringsend in the seventeenth century. A description of 'Riding the Franchises' in 1488 mentions 'Ring's-end' but this description does not mention inhabitants in this area.[3] It might have been a landing place, though, from very early on.

> Galleys of the Lochlanns ran here to beach, in quest of prey, their bloodbeaked prows riding low on a molten pewter surf. Danevikings, torcs of tomahawks aglitter on their breasts when Malachi wore the collar of gold.[4]

The reference to Malachi indicates the time. Two Irish high kings had that name: Malachi I (Máel Sechnaill mac Máele Ruanaid) died 27 November 862, and Malachi II (Máel Sechnaill mac Domnaill) lived 948–1022. The reference to the coming of the Vikings points to Malachi I. It should be mentioned, however, that the quoted author had a good reputation as a singer and an even better one as a wizard with words, but he cannot be thought a reliable source for historical facts as the people of Lochlann (meaning Scandinavia, especially Norway) did not have 'galleys' – or 'tomahawks'.

A second – similarly fanciful – quote talks about Ringsend as a town at a time 300 years later than the first. It was allegedly made by one of Ringsend's 'nobility', a lady whose father was according to her 'a boatbuilder beyond at Ringsend' and when questioned if he really was a boatbuilder she replied, 'Yes. In Ringsend, a town that thrun back Strongbow and send him on to Dublin.' [5]

NORMAN CONQUEST

When the Normans arrived in Ireland from Wales, their leader was the Cambro-Norman knight-adventurer Richard FitzGilbert de Clare, Earl of Strigoil (modern Chepstow), like his father nicknamed 'Arc-Fort'

(Strongbow). His father had been Earl of Pembroke, but this title was not conferred on the son by King Henry II. This was probably in retaliation for the fact that in the struggle between King Stephen and the Empress Maud both father and son had supported Stephen against Maud, the mother of the later established king, Henry II. Strongbow had some disputes with his overlord Henry II FitzEmpress, King of England, Duke of Normandy and Aquitaine, Count of Anjou, Maine and Nantes (and probably many more minor titles, especially in France), concerning the Irish lands he had conquered. As Strongbow had married Aoife, the daughter of Diarmaid MacMurchada, King of Leinster, he had, according to Norman law, inherited the right to rule Leinster, including the city of Dublin, after Diarmaid's death. King Henry II was afraid that his vassal might conquer even more land and eventually make himself King of Ireland; therefore he forced him to hand Dublin over to his king, but let him keep Leinster as lordship under the king's suzerainty.

Strongbow himself then granted some of this land to other adventurer-knights who had accompanied him to Ireland. The best part of the coastal area as well as stretches of Kildare went to Walter de Ridelesford[6] in grateful acknowledgment that this knight had killed John de Wode, a fierce warrior and one of the important jarls that had come to support the Norse king of Dublin against the Normans. At least that is what stories about de Ridelesford say.

Walter de Ridelesford, who was subsequently referred to as Lord of Bray, was married to Amabilis, daughter of Henry FitzRoi and thus a granddaughter of King Henry I. She was also half-sister of Meiler FitzHenry, the first Justiciar of Ireland. Walter de Ridelesford's son and heir, also named Walter de Ridelesford, and his wife donated part of their land unconditionally to the Priory of All Hallows[7] and another 39 acres to the same priory for the rent of one pound of pepper annually.[8]

2

RINGSEND

THE NAME

The name 'Ringsend' sounds like a combination of an Irish and an English word. The Irish word 'rinn' means 'point, headland' and is used to describe the end of the narrow peninsula between the Dodder and the sea. The name was mocked by some English writers who did not know the background and pointed out the stupidity of the Irish not knowing that rings had no end.

Those writers were not prepared to understand that the first part of the name was not the English word 'ring'. Actually the second part of the name of Ringsend also has nothing to do with an English word. The '-end' part was a corruption of another Irish word. According to S. Lewis, the name originally was Rin-aun (modern Rinn-ann):

> This place, according to O'Halloran, was originally called Rin-Aun, signifying in the Irish language, 'the point of the tide', from its situation on the confluence of the Dodder with the Liffey; its present name is a singular corruption of the former ...[1]

Some years ago there still was an old signpost on the way to Ringsend from the city and ahead of the bridge across the Dodder, pointing towards the sea and bearing the inscription 'Rinn Muirbhthean' (the Point of Merrion).

RINGSEND HISTORY: PIGEON HOUSE AND SOUTH WALL

Ringsend was a landing place for people and some goods since at least the fourteenth century.[2] This does not necessarily mean that people lived permanently there; it might just have been a place where goods and people disembarked for Dublin.

Later bigger ships with goods for Dublin anchored in Dalkey Sound, but this seems to have changed again around the end of the sixteenth century. From that time Ringsend was regarded as the official harbour for Dublin[3] and many people will know that Oliver Cromwell landed there in 1649. Less well known is what D'Alton says about this event, quoting the memoirs of Edmund Ludlow (1698):

> On his arrival in the bay of Dublin the men-of-war that accompanied him, and other ships in the harbour, rung such a peal with their cannon, as if some great news had been coming. He and his company went up in boats to the Ringsend, where they went ashore, and were met by most of the officers, civil and military, about the town; the end of his coming over was not at first discovered, and conjectured to be only to command in the army as major-general under Fleetwood.[4]

The expression that they 'went in boats to the Ringsend' indicates that 'the Ringsend' was a landing place, not a living place. At those times ships at the Ringsend did not moor at a wharf, but anchored in 'Poolbeg' (from the Irish 'poll beag', meaning a small deep place).

Around that time a wall alongside the Liffey to the mouth of the Dodder was built. This is now known as Sir John Rogerson's Quay. The 'harbour' or better the anchoring place Poolbeg can be identified in the engraving by the agglomeration of ships in the bay near the then existing village of Ringsend. Even when the South Wall had been built further out and was nearly finished, it could have happened that part of it gave way and the land that had been reclaimed behind it became submerged again. This occurred for instance in January 1792 when the Duke of Leinster managed to sail with his yacht across the flooded South Lotts and moor behind his house (Leinster House) in what was to become Merrion Square. The 1745 engraving of the view from Beggars' Bush shows also that Ringsend and Irishtown were separate entities with the majority of buildings in Ringsend and with St Matthew's Church in Irishtown just appearing at the right edge of the engraving.

To get from the port in Ringsend to Dublin was not easy, as the Dodder had to be crossed. Even today this river still is not completely tamed, but in the seventeenth century not much effort had been made even to try to do so. Bridges across it had been built since at least 1640 and probably much earlier, most of them much further upriver as in Ballsbridge, Donnybrook and even Clonskeagh, but many were destroyed by floods. In Ringsend the

View of Ringsend, Irish Town, Pool Beg, Clontarf, Irelands-Eye, Dublin Bay, &c. in IRELAND.

The view from Beggars' Bush, c. 1745.

Dodder could be crossed at low tide in a 'Ringsend Car', which was a horse drawn vehicle with a seat suspended between two wheels which had wide rims to prevent them from sinking into the wet sand.

From the seventeenth century on many harbour officials and custom officers lived in Ringsend. Most of them were English and members of the established church. As their way to the parish church in Donnybrook was often impassable because of the frequent floodings of the area by the Dodder, they applied for a chapel to be built near them. Their request was granted by King William III. After his death Queen Anne became the patron of the church. This made the church a Royal Chapel, and so its official name is 'Royal Chapel of St Matthew's in Ringsend'. Despite that name it is situated in Irishtown and will be described with that village.

Samuel Lewis[5] describes Ringsend in 1837 as a small town. Revd Beaver H. Blacker quotes the 1851 census giving 2,064 inhabitants for Ringsend without Irishtown.[6] In 1863 Ringsend had 1,931 inhabitants in 209 (often dilapidated) houses.[7] The impression of a town might not only have come from the number of inhabitants, but would also have been boosted by the presence of the garrison in Pigeonhouse Fort, halfway along the South Wall nearby.

The Great South Wall, built in the second half of the eighteenth century, was the longest sea wall in Europe and still is one of the longest, though land reclamation hides that fact to some extent.

> From the 'Point' of Ringsend, the South-wall extends into the bay 17,754 feet; nearly three English miles and an half. It was commenced in 1748, and finally completed in 1796; and is composed of blocks of mountain granite, strongly cemented, and strengthened with iron cramps. The breadth of the road to a strong artillery station called the Pigeon-house (which was erected near the close of the last century, and is 7,938 feet from Ringsend), is nearly forty feet at bottom, but narrows to twenty-eight feet at top; the whole rising five feet above high-water. There is a basin at the former place, 900 feet long by 450 broad, and a landing-place raised 200 feet broad, on which are several convenient wharfs, not but little frequented. The pier at this point is 250 feet wide; and on it are raised buildings, which were formerly used as a magazine, an arsenal, and a custom-house. In the channel between the Pigeon-house and the Light-house is the anchorage called Poolbeg (formerly denominated Cleer-rode, Clareroad, and Clarade) where vessels may lie in fifteen feet at low water. At the extremity of the Wall is the Light-house, commenced in 1761, and completed in 1768, under considerable difficulties, by Mr Smith.[8]

The nautical expression 'cleer-rode' today is hardly known by anybody who is not involved in shipping. The word is composed of two parts which in modern English would be 'clear' in the sense of 'safe' added to the nautical expression 'road' (compare French 'rade' and German 'Reede'). A 'road' in this sense is a place where ships can anchor, though without shelter. As a nautical term this word is still used with the same meaning nowadays.

D'Alton described the South Wall in exactly the same words that Revd Blacker used, but D'Alton then goes on to explain the difficulties in building the lighthouse:

> … from the depth of water, the raging of the seas, and the power of the winds in such an exposed situation. Those obstacles, however, were

overcome by the skill of Mr Smyth, the architect, who collected vast rocks, and deposited them in a huge caissoon or chest, which was sunk to the bed of the sea, and afterwards guarded with a buttress of solid masonry, twenty-five feet broad at the base. On this the ingenious architect raised a beautiful circular structure, three stories high, surrounded by an octagonal lanthorn of eight windows.[9]

This lighthouse at the end of the Great South Wall replaced a former lightship that had shown the entrance to Dublin's harbour since 1735.[10] When the lighthouse was finished nearly two hundred and fifty years ago, it did not look like it does today.

This was the first lighthouse in the world to be illuminated by candlepower, and from 1786 on it was one of the first using spermaceti oil (a clear, yellowish liquid produced by the sperm whale) as lamp fuel. Hook Lighthouse in Co. Wexford changed to spermaceti oil five years later in 1791.

In the second half of the nineteenth century it was decided to secure the base of the lighthouse by laying reinforced concrete blocks around it. This work was done using the diving bell that the port engineer of that time, Bindon Blood Stoney, had introduced in 1860 for underwater port work.

This diving bell has been preserved and today (2017) can be inspected on Sir John Rogerson's Quay.

First Poolbeg Lighthouse, finished 1768. (From N. Whittock, *A Picturesque Guide Through Dublin* (Dublin 1846))

Poolbeg
Lighthouse
and old
crane.

Poolbeg Lighthouse now is electrified and automated. It used to have a foghorn as well, but this was switched off some years ago. Until then its booming sound told all inhabitants up to a few kilometres away that the visibility at sea was bad, even when it might have been a clear day on land. People living near it were not pleased, though, when it went off in the middle of the night.

The full length of the South Wall is more than five kilometres from the original start to the lighthouse at the tip. When the Poolbeg Peninsula was reclaimed from the sea, the new land made the wall look shorter. Because of modern land reclamation only a part of the original wall has water on both sides: the River Liffey on the left and the sea on the right when facing outwards.

Dublin citizens, for whom the South Wall was a favourite place for walks, had occasion to complain in 1766 that it was not very pleasing to walk there. In December 1765 or as other reports say on 4 March 1766, four men were hanged at the gallows that at that time was near Baggotrath Castle. What happened afterwards is explained by Gaskin:

The following note appears in all the Dublin papers of 9 March 1766:

The bodies of the four murderers and pirates – McKinley, St Quinton, Gidley, and Zekerman, were brought in the black cart from Newgate, and hung in chains, two of them near Mackarell's Wharf, on the South Wall near Ringsend, and the other two about the Middle of the Piles, below the Pigeon House.

The bodies of the four pirates remained suspended on the wharf and at the Pigeon House till the month of March following. On 11 March, however, a letter appeared in Faulkner's Journal, signed a 'Freeholder', complaining of the hoops which bound the bodies as being very imperfect. On referring to the same journal for 29 March I find the following:

The two pirates, Peter McKinley and George Gidley, who hang in chains on the South Wall for the murder of Captain Coghlan, etc., being very disagreeable to the citizens who walk there for amusement and health, are immediately to be put on Dalkey Island, for which purpose new irons are being made, those they hang in being faulty. Richard St Quintan and Andrea Zekerman, the other two concerned in this cruel affairs, are to remain on the Piles at the Pigeon House.' Accordingly the same journal, on the 1st and 12th of April, 1767, announces the removal of the bodies, in deference to public opinion, from the new wall, and that they were carried by sea to the rock on the Muglins, near Dalkey Island, where a gibbet was erected and they were hung up in irons, said to be the completest ever made in the kingdom.[11]

At the end of the eighteenth century the packet boats went to and from Poolbeg Harbour, then partly protected by the South Wall. A Mr Pidgeon was employed as caretaker for a house built to store material that was used in the harbour. In due course Mr Pidgeon discovered that he could earn extra money by providing food for the passengers arriving and leaving, and for Dubliners just coming out for the day to watch whatever was happening. The house later turned into a hotel and the name changed to Pigeon. In 1813 the War Office bought Pigeon House Hotel, together with other buildings and the ground around them from the Harbour Commissioners for slightly more than £100,000 and built a fortress a short stretch west of the Half Moon Battery on the South Wall.[12] When it finally dawned to the authorities that Napoleon would not attack Dublin and that even later in the nineteenth century nobody else had such ideas, the fortress was dismantled and sold to Dublin Corporation in 1897 for £65,000.[13]

Pigeon House Hotel is still there, though now it is neither a hotel, storeroom nor part of a fort. It is surrounded by industrial buildings and its distinctive back with the two semi-circular wings on either side is not easy to see. The guns are part of the few remains of the fort.

The Pigeon House Fort was planned to protect the harbour, but also to safeguard bullion and important documents. The only part left is the ruin of the entrance. It is not clear why the cannons that still exist aim towards the fort instead of away from it.

The remains of the entrance to Pigeon House Fort.

The South Wall used to house another institution: the Isolation Hospital. This had in 1903 replaced the Hospital Ship that had been anchored nearby since 1874. Both the hospital ship as well as the hospital were meant for treating people with cholera (and possibly other infectious diseases), thus removing them from town. Different sources mention a hospital in this area under the names: 'Isolation Hospital', 'Cholera Hospital', 'Pigeon House Sanatorium', 'St. Catherine's Hospital', 'Alan A. Ryan Home – Hospital for advanced cases'. They all seem to be the same place that is mentioned on the 1907 OS map as 'Isolation Hospital'. The Pigeon House Sanatorium for patients with tuberculosis was part of the campaign of the Countess of Aberdeen, wife of the then Lord Lieutenant, who fought against this illness. Her hospital opened in 1907.[14] This hospital, situated west of the electricity station and the sewage works, is described in the Environmental Appraisal of the Dublin Waste to Energy Project as St Catherine's Hospital.[15] One building of the 1907 complex is still extant. The former complex included a Roman Catholic chapel and a convent with other buildings. Those have disappeared. The modern yellow steel door in the wall shows the address '85c Pigeonhouse Road'. This is the address of a firm of analytical services.

RINGSEND HISTORY: THE VILLAGE

The first buildings of the village of Ringsend appeared east of the mouth of the Dodder (left on the photograph) and that is where the centre of Ringsend still is, even though it keeps changing.

In general the Grand Canal was and is regarded as the border between Pembroke, Dublin 4, and Dublin Inner City. At the Grand Canal Basin, however, the border originally ran along the middle of Barrow Street, leaving the warehouses on the canal outside Pembroke Township.

Grand Canal Basin is accessed from the mouth of the Liffey through three locks named (from west to east) Westmoreland Lock, Buckingham Lock and Camden Lock. The size of the locks increases from west to east. Nowadays only Camden Lock is still in use.

The road from the locks to Ringsend runs directly beside the Dodder and shows that the course of this still quite tempestuous river has been straightened. Much could be done in this area to make it into a nice little water side park.

The mouth of the Dodder, 2010.

Camden Lock at Grand Canal Dock.

Freshly painted Victorian letterbox in Ringsend.

The reason why Ringsend – one of the poorer districts in the surroundings of Dublin – got a letterbox as early as during the reign of Queen Victoria is most likely because of the garrison that was housed there. This letterbox is situated at the corner of Bridge Street and Thorncastle Street, in front of the house that used to be the post office.

AN RINN

An Rinn, the tip of the long and narrow peninsula between the Dodder and Liffey rivers is the oldest part of Ringsend. This is the location of Cambridge House, situated on Cambridge Road between St Patrick's Boys' and Girls' national schools on the one side and Ringsend Technical School on the other side. Cambridge Road and York Road both were named in the second half of the nineteenth century after the Duke of Cambridge and the Duke of York, both younger sons of George III. The title Duke of York is traditionally given to the second son of the reigning monarch. The person after whom this street

Cambridge
House.

in Ringsend was named, was Frederick Augustus, second son of George III. He held the position of Commander-in-Chief of the British Army for many years and was the original 'Grand old Duke of York' of the well-known children's rhyme. Cambridge Road was either named after the seventh son of George III or after this prince's son.

Cambridge House is situated in an area that was still a tidal mudflat in 1837. The house is shown on the OS map of 1907. For some time it was occupied by the Health Service and later it functioned as Ringsend Regional Office of Dublin City Council. In autumn 2016 it housed a crèche.

An Rinn features an enigmatic structure beside the clubhouse of St Patrick's Rowing Club on York Road, just opposite the end of Thorncastle Street. It looks a bit like one of the old tram posts that later were used for street lamps, but there is no lamp attached to this one. It is inscribed:

(front):

S. D.
R. D. C.

(back):

1909

A member of the rowing club explained that it was a ventilation shaft. The inscription 'S. D. R. D. C.' stands for 'South Dublin Rural District

Council'. The Rural District South Dublin was more or less the area that now is the county of Dún Laoghaire-Rathdown. How this shaft came to be in Ringsend is not known. If it really was used for ventilation, it was most likely connected to the sewage system, which includes a sewage canal under the Liffey.[16] This was only built between 1926 and 1928 and the post gives the date 1909, so it must have done duty somewhere else in its first years.

From this spot the view across the Liffey at nighttime shows some modern illuminated structures. One of these structures does not exist anymore. 'The Revolver', Dublin's version of the Big Wheel at the Point, just opposite Ringsend, did not last very long. It was opened in July 2010 and dismantled in November 2011.

Another structure is the International Conference Centre. At nighttime the light bands around the part of it that looks like a huge tilted barrel sometimes run in changing colours.

In Ringsend, as elsewhere along the Dodder, bridges were often damaged by the force of the river. For Ringsend that meant difficulties getting to Dublin. Sometimes an enterprising firm found a solution, as Richard Lewis reports:

> Ferry-boats ply also occasionally, but constantly on Sundays, between the lower end of Aston's-quay and Ringsend, at the rate of a penny for each passenger.[17]

Another possibility was to use 'Ringsend cars', unique two-wheeled horse-drawn vehicles with one axle and a seat suspended on leather straps between the two wheels. The wheels were wide so that they would not sink into the wet and sometimes soft ground around the Dodder. Still, they could only be used at low tide and not at all when the Dodder was in flood.

The maritime age of Ringsend is not over, although activities have moved further east, where a huge container port makes the life of the people living in the cottages of Pigeon House Road much more uncomfortable than it used to be. Memories remain of former times, when fishing boats and ferries were active in the area.

There are other memories, preserved through sport. The 'Hobblers' Challenge' is a competition of the coastal rowing clubs on the east coast, which will row out from the Hobblers' Monument in Dún Laoghaire to the Kish Bank Lighthouse and back. In 2010, but also in other years, this was won by the Ringsend Stella Maris Rowing Club.

At the Dodder's bank in Ringsend, 2008.

THE CENTRE OF RINGSEND

In 1893 small 'artisan' cottages for fishermen and craftsmen were built between Ringsend College and the village centre. As the water of Liffey and Dodder were definitely not of drinking water quality, a fresh water fountain was erected in 1906, something that was not usual at those times. Ringsend Park cottages behind this fountain were built in 1922.

Some of the earlier cottages have rather wide doors. Perhaps originally the craftsmen were not only living but also working in those cottages and needed a wider entrance for goods deliveries.

Most of Ringsend's shops are found around St Patrick's Church just south of the bridge on Bridge Street, Thorncastle Street and Fitzwilliam Street. The street sign shows that the Fitzwilliam family, though they regarded themselves as English and hardly ever stayed on their estate in Ireland, did not mind that their name was translated into Irish as Mac Liam. They always were regarded as good landlords by their tenants.

Bridge Street still has old houses, but the southern end of Fitzwilliam Street, behind Ringsend Library, has been refurbished with new buildings

Drinking
fountain at
the corner of
Ringsend Park.

and modern shops. On the other side of the library there are older and
more traditional shops as well, mainly small and sometimes crammed with
merchandise but also with a cosy feel.

Ringsend Market was originally a typical village greengrocer's shop. In
summer 2015 it had transformed to a butcher's and fifteen months later it
had become a florist's shop. It might change again but it is to be hoped that
it always will remain a typical village shop.

Because of the unpredictable Dodder there often were problems, especially
concerning transport from Ringsend, the mooring place for ships, to Dublin,
the destination of passengers and goods. Many Dodder bridges have been
destroyed by the river, not only in Ringsend, but also further upriver. At
times the first bridge crossing the Dodder was in Clonskeagh, 5km upstream
from Ringsend. Ringsend itself is said to have had bridges destroyed in
1739, 1782, 1786 and 1802. In some of those cases it is not clear, though,
if those bridges were situated in the village of Ringsend or if they only
served Ringsend and were, perhaps, situated in Ballsbridge. For many years
Ringsend had no bridge at all and Ringsend people had to be content with
makeshift solutions.

The main reason for the destruction of the older bridges was that the River
Dodder had a wide delta at Ringsend and the ground was not very stable.
It was only at the beginning of the nineteenth century that a lasting bridge
finally was erected. This still existing bridge was opened in 1812 and named
Charlotte Bridge after Princess Charlotte, daughter of the Prince Regent. Few
use that name, however, and the bridge was and is always simply referred

Ringsend 'Bridge' (after a drawing by John James Barralet 1787).

Ringsend Bridge at low tide.

to as Ringsend Bridge. It survived because it is not like other bridges with pillars on foundations at the river's edge and therefore not necessarily very stable. This bridge is an elliptical pipe as can be seen at low tide (the Dodder is tidal up to Ballsbridge).

Ringsend Road on the west side of the bridge and Bridge Street on the east side have both been widened, but as Ringsend Bridge is a protected structure, it cannot be changed. Any car driver coming from Dublin will find it difficult to observe traffic turning towards the city from Fitzwilliam Quay on the other side of the river. Occasionally that can lead to problems, but by far the biggest problems still are caused by the river flooding.

In the beginning of 2011 a flood undermined the wall beside the Dodder on Fitzwilliam Quay at the edge of Ringsend Bridge and the wall collapsed. It took many months until this damage was finally repaired.

FURTHER IMPRESSIONS

Richard Lewis wrote about Ringsend after a storm had damaged it:

> Ringsend was greatly frequented some years ago, but is now in a melancholy situation. It appears like a town that has experienced the calamities of war, that has been sacked by an enemy, and felt the depredations of all-conquering Time. There are, however, some good places of entertainment for the accommodation of the Citizens of Dublin and strangers who visit it; among which the tavern on the right hand of the place where the Bridge stood, kept by HARRISON, ranks the foremost.[18]

Despite industrialisation with chemical factories, glass works, mills and others, a connection with the sea can still be detected – for instance in the names of places of hospitality. (All houses in Dublin and surroundings change the colour of their facades regularly, so the photographed buildings might look different now.)

This is by far not the only reference to fishing, the sea or boating in Ringsend.

Thom's Directory for 1862 notes a spirit and beer dealer and three vintners in Bridge Street and three vintners in Thorncastle Street, among them J. Nickolls of the 'Old England' and Edward Egan. In 1868 the 'Yacht' of No. 67 Thorncastle Street was owned by Joseph Egan and J. Mulholland is mentioned as owning the 'Old England'.

B & B in the centre of Ringsend.

'The Yacht' in Ringsend has been in the same spot since 1868 at least.

An increase in sea traffic created a new source of income for the Ringsend men who knew all the shifting sandbanks in Dublin Bay. Whenever a schooner or steamship arrived, the hobblers set out from Ringsend and from Dún Laoghaire. Usually four men per boat, often from the same family, they rowed or sailed out towards the ship they had seen. The first boat that reached the ship would get the contract to pilot her into a safe anchoring place and more often than not also the contract to help discharge the cargo.

Hobbling was banned by the Port and Docks Board in 1936. Gerry Brannocks of Stella Maris Rowing Club in Ringsend relates how his father-in-law had been one of the last hobblers in Ringsend. This hobbler had a friend in Wexford, who when he discovered a schooner or steamer going north towards Dublin would send a telegram to his friend. The hobbler then had to use his knowledge of weather, wind and tide to work out when the advised boat would be near enough to be reached by his hobbling team. Knowing of the arrival would give him an advantage over the competing hobblers from Dún Laoghaire.

Hobbling was a dangerous business as the men had to go out in any weather. More than once a boat did not come back. One of the last instances is documented:

> On the morning of the 6th December 1934 the people of Dún Laoghaire and Ringsend were shocked to learn of the drowning of three young Dún Laoghaire hobblers in Dublin Bay on the previous evening. The three young men were the brothers Richard (18) and Henry (20) Shortall and their companion John Hughes. A fourth member of the crew owes his life to the fact that he remained behind in Dublin Port to collect money owed to them for piloting and mooring a ship at the North Wall. He was Gareth Hughes, a brother of John. The Shortall brothers came from a family of twelve and resided in Clarence Street. They were on their way home when their skiff ran into an east-south-east wind. It was a situation they had encountered on many previous occasions and they were strong, able and experienced boatmen. Their boat, *The Jealous of Me*, was last seen by the lighthouse men as it sailed past the Poolbeg at dusk. What went wrong on that fateful night will never be known. On the morning of the 6th of December it was found washed ashore at the Irishtown Gate at Ringsend Park. The local people realised that a terrible disaster had occurred. A few days later the bodies of the Shortall brothers were recovered from the sea and later laid to rest in Dean's Grange Cemetery. Unfortunately, the body of John Hughes was never found.[19]

After this report the name of the Hobbler's End pub seemed callous, but it was definitely not intentional. At the end of his working day the hobbler surely would need some relaxation and it is indicated where he might get it in the evening of a strenuous day.

Over the years this pub changed hands and name a few times. At the turn of the millennium it traded under the name Bunit & Simpson, not because those were the names of the licensees, but in memory of the firm that had leased the Poolbeg oyster fishery in the mid-eighteenth century. Like many other pubs in Dublin it has seen good and bad times. Not so long ago it was refurbished and combined with another pub.

In earlier times the pub beside it had taken up the nickname of 'Ringsend'. Ringsend was often called 'Raytown' in a rather derogatory way, but the Ringsend people turned it into something to be proud of. This pub now has changed hands and also the name.

Some of the pubs on Bridge Street have ceased trading, while others have consolidated. Raytown Bar and Hobbler's End have merged into one pub with the new name South Dock, and the Oarsman incorporated the shop that had existed beside it in earlier years.

Samuel Lewis, in his *Topographical Dictionary*,[20] calls Ringsend together with Irishtown 'a small town' and even nowadays, nearly 200 years later, it does have the look of a small country town with its shops and pubs, its

Bridge Street, Ringsend.

church, its technical college, its library and its post office, though the latter has moved lately into a more modern part of Ringsend.

CONNECTIONS WITH THE SEA: FISHING, SHIPPING AND COASTGUARD

According to the history of the area accepted by most, Ringsend village began its life as a fishing village in the sixteenth or at latest in the seventeenth century. Some historians might push the time for the origins of Ringsend back to the tenth century, though their reasoning seems rather subjective. Whatever the century might have been in which Ringsend grew into a (fishing) village, not everyone who had a boat and a net, or a line with a hook was allowed to fish. Fishing was regulated; the fishing rights belonged to the landlord who could lease them to a tenant or keep them for himself, even when the land at the shore was leased to somebody else. After the de Ridelesford family had died out and their land had fallen to the Crown, Thorncastle was leased to William le Deveney in 1299, including the fishing rights. Later the Fitzwilliams owned the fishing rights from Ringsend southwards to Booterstown, and they either kept them for themselves when they leased the land or included an amount of fish in the annual rent. On the mouth of the Dodder and on the Liffey the fishing rights seem to have been state owned, at least in the Middle Ages.

> AD 1331. A great famine afflicted all Ireland in this and the foregoing year, and the city of Dublin suffered miserably. But the people in their distress met with an unexpected and providential relief. For about the 24th of June a prodigious number of large sea fish, called Turlehydes, were brought into the bay of Dublin, and cast on shore at the mouth of the river Dodder (This is now called Donebrook river, and falls into the Liffey at Ringsend). They were from 30 to 40 feet long and so bulky, that two tall men placed one on each side of the fish could not see one another. The lord justice, Sir Anthony Lucy, with his servants, and many of the citizens of Dublin, killed about 200 of them, and gave leave to the poor to carry them away at their pleasure.[21]

In *The Dublin Region in the Middle Ages* these fish were referred to as pilot whales.[22] Pilot whales have a rather pronounced round head which gives them their scientific name '*globicephala melas*' which translates as 'Black Globehead'. They belong to the Dolphin group and together with killer whales are the biggest members of this group. Pilot whales usually occur in big schools and are relatively often found beached.

Apart from herring, ray and other fish, Ringsend was well known for its shellfish, including oysters. The oyster fishery was leased as the following newspaper excerpt of 1748 shows: 'Poolbeg oyster fishery being taken this year by Messrs. Bunit and Simpson of Ringsend, they may be had fresh in their purity at Mrs L'Sware's at the sign of the *Good Woman* in Ringsend aforesaid.'[23]

The sign of the *Good Woman* could indicate a public house, but also a fishmonger, victualler or grocer, especially as the two latter ones often were connected with a pub. Before house numbers were known, the 'address' of a business was given by a sign over the door.

Considering herrings, D'Alton says about the herrings in Dublin Bay: 'The herrings caught in this bay are highly esteemed as more sweet and oily than those from Wales or Scotland.'[24] Today herrings, shrimp and oysters all have disappeared from this part of Dublin Bay. Herrings were overfished, shrimp were killed in 'The Big Frost', an especially severe winter in 1740 and never found their way back, and as far as oysters are concerned, they need much less polluted water than could be found in Dublin Bay during past centuries.

Boat building was a big industry in Ringsend from the eighteenth into the third quarter of the twentieth century, though it had started even earlier. In the seventeenth century Sir William Petty (of the Down Survey) was interested in a new design for boats and had the idea of building twin-hulled boats, nowadays known as catamarans. The first boat of this design was launched on 22 December 1662, at what now is Wolfe Tone Quay. She won the world's first recorded open yacht race, held in Dublin Bay on 6 January 1663. In 1684 a boat of the same design was built in Ringsend.[25]

The 1837 OS map only lists one 'slip', just north of Ringsend Bridge on the right bank of the Dodder. The 1907 OS map shows a boat slip at the same spot but also nine more boat slips between the bridge and the mouth of the Dodder, some of which might have been those of a number of rowing clubs that had started to appear in Ringsend from the 1830s. North of the boat slips the map also shows a landing stage (at the coal yard) and a 'wooden pier'.

In 1800 the Ballast Board employed John Clement of Ringsend to build a lifeboat to be stationed in Clontarf. In 1803 a second of Clement's boats went to Sandycove, a third to Sutton in 1805 and another one to Poolbeg in 1815. John Clement was not the only boat builder. Pat Sweeney mentions King's Shipyard, John Marshall, Courtney Clarke, Barrington's, Henry Teal and Richard Weldrick as shipbuilding firms in Ringsend in the nineteenth century. Most of them were situated in Thorncastle Street.[26] Shipbuilding continued into the twentieth century:

> In 1920 the Corporation ordered new motor ferries to be built in the boat building yard of John Hollwey at Ringsend.[27]

Ringsend ship- and boatyards have disappeared. O'Rahilly House and Whelan House were built on sites where boats had been built before. Even the street name King's Yard, later called Thorncastle Place, does not exist anymore, though a memory still seems to linger on the end wall of the canal basin as seen from the western bank of Grand Canal Dock. The word 'Kings' is clearly in view and the entrance to one of the originally three former dry docks can just be made out.

According to Pat Sweeney[28] a survey of the British Admiralty in 1805 found no shipwrights over the age of 50 years in Ireland. The work of a shipwright was physically very demanding and at the age of 50 any shipwright who had not been killed or disabled in a work-related accident would be what nowadays is described as 'burnt-out'.

Ringsend Dockyard Company (Dublin) Ltd, sometimes referred to as (William) McMullan's after its early owner, was founded in 1913.[29] This company built (small) ships and they were well known for their repairing work. They went out of business in 1963.

Murphy's was probably the last of the boatbuilders in Thorncastle Street, Ringsend. Murphy's boatyard might have started as early as the eighteenth century when a shipwright at Sir John Rogerson's Quay, Hugh Murphy, built a boat for the Ballast Board. The boatyard of the Murphy family was closed in 1950. Joe Murphy, however, who was born in Ringsend in 1928 and died there in 2011, had been working with his father in that boatyard and kept on building boats for his friends nearly until his death, long after the boatyard itself was closed.[30]

Boatbuilding still has not stopped completely in Ringsend. In 1991 a replica of Sir William Petty's catamaran, which had been named *St Michael*, was built at the Irish Nautical Trusts premises at the Grand Canal Basin in Ringsend and given the name *Simon and Jude*, rounding up over 300 years of shipbuilding in Ringsend. The same trust bought the old Aran Island ferry *Naomh Éanna*, moored at Charlotte Quay, restored it and used it as a micro-enterprise centre. The *Naomh Éanna* was a CIE ferry that ran between Galway and the Aran Islands from the 1950s until 1986. The author himself has been on board her, returning from Inis Mór to Galway in the early 1970s.

It had been planned to use the *Naomh Éanna* and the former lifeboat *Mary Stanford* as a nucleus for a Floating Maritime Museum.[31] Unfortunately the plans failed, mainly due to lack of financial support. At the beginning of 2015 the *Naomh Éanna* rested in one of the restored graving docks at the east end of Grand Canal Basin and awaited an uncertain future.

Boat building implies other industries, like for instance rope-making. The 1837 OS map shows two short rope walks, one at Charlotte Quay and the other near the beginning of the South Wall. Apart from those the map also shows a longer rope walk at the edge of the sea along the whole stretch from Ringsend to the border of Irishtown townland, shortly before Murphy's Baths. The 1907 OS map shows a street named 'Rope Walk Place'. This street is still there and still has the same name, going from Fitzwilliam Street to what then was the edge of the sea and now is the western edge of Ringsend Park.

Rope-making was still a going concern in Ringsend until the mid-twentieth century.[32] In 1907 there were rope works recorded between the gasworks and Gordon Street in the South Lotts according to the OS map of that year. This area had not been a part of Pembroke Township then, but now it is regarded as a part of Ringsend.

Naomh Éanna in graving dock, Grand Canal Basin.

Coastguard houses, Ringsend.

Even though there is not much shipbuilding or fishing left in Ringsend; there are memories of naval times – for instance the buildings of the former coastguard station.

The first of the houses in the photograph, the one with the boathouse and tower, came onto the property market some years ago. According to the then description of the property the tower originally had its own entrance at ground floor. On this floor it could not be accessed from the rest of the house and it had its own staircase. There was, however, an entrance to it from the house on the first floor. The top room of the tower, with three windows facing in different directions was the watch room, whereas the ground floor was the coastguards' munitions room. As such it was raided by rebels looking for guns in 1921.[33] Described in the 2011 advertisement as 'needing some refurbishment', it at least then had a bathroom on the first floor. In general coastguard houses originally only had outdoor facilities.

Life as a coastguard was not easy, especially in a hostile environment like Ringsend. In the nineteenth century the coastguard was run in a style similar to the navy, with only rather Spartan furniture in each house, but for that the inventory included weapons.

Each home was allocated furniture, which included the following items:

One Iron Bedstead
One Table
Four Windsor Chairs
Two six foot Forms
One Coal Box to hold half bushel of coal
Fire Irons, Fender
Musket, Bayonet
Pistol and Two Sea Service pistols.[34]

The coastguard men had to keep everything in order, while their wives had to grow vegetables in the little garden plots behind the houses and do their washing in the communal wash house. Watch duty went from 4.30 p.m. to 8 a.m. in all weathers. Absence through sickness was frequent, but when sick a coastguard man received only two thirds of his normal pay.

Today the Irish Coast Guard is a Division of the Department of Transport and is responsible for maritime safety and search and rescue. When it was founded in 1822 it had another function: revenue protection. The rather big coastguard station in Ringsend points to another 'industry' for Ringsend people in the nineteenth century: like the fishing harbours of north county Dublin they were involved in much contraband trading – especially in tobacco and spirits.

OTHER INDUSTRIES

In the eighteenth century, and possibly even earlier, Ringsend had salt works, probably because of the fishing industry and the necessity to victual ships calling there. In the nineteenth century there was also an iron foundry (or possibly more than one). K.A. Murray mentions that three Cornish boilers for the Atmospheric Railway in Dalkey were made at the Ringsend Ironworks.[35]

In the latter part of the eighteenth century Ringsend fell into a decline. After the port had been moved first to Howth and then to Kingstown (Dún Laoghaire), Ringsend was described by various people in the first half of the nineteenth century as the dirtiest village at the outskirts of Dublin. The proximity to sea and canal had attracted different types of factories. After the harbour and custom officials were gone, most of the inhabitants would have been labourers, and as quite a number of the factories were short-lived, many

Ringsend people were without work. In an 1833 questionnaire of the Royal Commission into the state of the Irish poor, the Roman Catholic parish priest of the parish of Donnybrook and Irishtown which included Ringsend, Dr Finn, mentioned Clarke's foundry, some salt works and still about twenty fishing boats and some ship carpenters.[36] Mother Mary Aikenhead wrote to the same commissioners that the foundry and the salt works were no longer flourishing and had curtailed their establishments in a great way. According to D'Alton[37] this foundry had employed fifty men. Mother Aikenhead mentioned that the glass works that had been there earlier had closed in May 1833.[38]

Ringsend was quite important for glassmaking in the Dublin area for more than 200 years. An English firm had established a glassmaking factory there around 1787, mainly catering for the French market. This market would have been lost for the Ringsend works after the French Revolution. The glassworks were supposed to have closed in 1833, but the 1837 OS map shows a building in Ringsend with the words 'Glass Works' beside it. Around forty years later glassworks were established to make sheet glass and glass containers. These works stopped the production of sheet glass in the 1950s and concentrated wholly on glass bottles, taking up an earlier tradition. The OS map of 1907 shows a 'Bottle Factory' and 'Glass Works' filling the area between Grand Canal Dock in the north, South Dock Road in the east, Ringsend Road in the south and the 'Tram Power Station' in the west. Apart from that the map shows 'Glass Works' at the corner of Fitzwilliam Quay and Riverview Avenue (now Dermot O'Hurley Avenue), 'Bottle Works' between the mouth of the Dodder and Thorncastle Street and smaller 'Bottle Works' between Cambridge Place (now disappeared, off Pembroke Cottages) and the 'Timber Yard' between Pembroke Cottages and Thorncastle Street. There also was a 'Bottle Factory' on the east side of Barrow Street, just north of South Dock Street.

A description of Leinster not long after the First World War mentions, 'The manufacture of glass bottles is carried on in Ringsend where there are three firms engaged in the work'.[39]

In the early years of the twentieth century (c. 1915) the glass bottle makers got their own 'club house', the Bottle Makers' Hall. They had up to six full size snooker tables in there, just for themselves. Other workers were only allowed in on special occasions, for instance to play 'Housey Housey' – nowadays called Bingo. This was played on leather squares that were marked off with chalk and later taken home to sole shoes.

According to the News Four 1997 Christmas edition the Bottle Makers' Hall was sold in the 1960s. Since then the overgrown front garden has been tidied up, but it is not clear what else will happen with this protected building.

For some time there also were chemical works in Ringsend. The 1837 map shows 'Dock Chemical Works' just north of the Dock Mills, a 'Salammoniac Factory' between Ringsend Road and Charlotte Quay, 'Lime and Salt Works' just north of the 'Salt Works' at the north-eastern corner of Ringsend and 'Lead Works' west of Fitzwilliam Street.

The 1868 edition of *Thom's Directory* mentions Pim's mills, Ringsend Salt Works, Ringsend Glass Bottle Company, the Dublin Dock Yard Company Shipbuilders and Frederick Barrington who describes himself as 'engineer, millwright, iron and brass founder, smith, and boiler maker, and iron ship builder, Ringsend Foundry'. Pat Sweeney mentions that Frederick Barrington was involved with others in the lease of the Grand Canal Basin, including the dry docks and that he had also taken over the operation of Camden and Buckingham Locks.[40]

When the Grand Canal Docks were opened, businesses that needed bulk material brought to them established themselves at the edge of the docks as transport by water was and still is the cheapest possible transport for mass goods. Even today there are buildings at the Ringsend side of Grand Canal Dock that can be recognised as former mills, though none of them are still functioning as mills today. Dock Mill is mentioned on the 1837 OS map of the area, just south of Dock Chemical Works. There still is a building on the same site, but this is now owned by Google and used as offices. Further north the map shows some buildings without inscription. Now there are six-storey high warehouses that according to one website were erected in the 1830s. In the 1860s these were part of the mills that belonged to the Pim brothers. These mills were taken over by Patrick Boland in 1873 and since then have been known as Boland's Mills, even though they stopped milling in 2001. The huge concrete silos of the 1940s have lately disappeared, as the whole area will be redeveloped. The old warehouses, however, will at least keep their outer shells, as these are protected structures.

Glass and bottlemaking as well as lead smelting are not without danger from heat, especially 130 years ago when safety measures were considered unimportant. On the other end of the temperature scale were the fishermen and hobblers who had to go out in wind and weather. It is no wonder that accidents and illnesses were frequent but this would not always stop the men working, as their families relied on their income. The Queen's Nurse in that district knew a lot about it. She had to treat '… severe scalds among the lead-smelters and glass-blowers, while the fishermen of course endured much cold and get laid up with inflammation of the lungs'.[41]

For some time there was a distillery in Ringsend. In 1834 the Dublin Directory lists 'Aeneas Coffey & Co, Dock Distillery, Grand Canal Street'.[42] Aeneas Coffey (1780–1852) started his career in the excise service where he worked his way up to Inspector General. During that time he often came into contact with illegal poitín distillers. Checking and dismantling those distilling apparatuses taught him a great deal about distilling. He resigned from the excise service in 1824 and bought or leased a small distillery at the above address in Ringsend. This distillery might possibly have been owned by Robert Haig of the Dodderbank Distillery in Sandymount before. Coffey's real interest was not distilling to sell drink, but to try out and improve his invention – the Coffey still – also known as patent still or columnar still. Coffey applied for the patent in 1830 and it was granted by King William IV in 1831. The still invented or at least vastly improved by Coffey works continuously, which the pot stills do not. On the other hand the Coffey still was so effective that it produced a rather flavourless distillate, which was the reason why his still was not accepted by most of Irish distillers.

The distillery worked under Coffey until 1839 but the original premises were sold to the Dublin and Kingstown Railway Co. and the 1837 OS map shows a 'Railway Coach Factory' on its ground. Before that Aeneas Coffey Senior and his son Aeneas Coffey Junior were listed as 'Aeneas Coffey, patent still manufacturer' at 3 Barrow Street.[43] The firm, established in 1830 in Dublin, had been completely taken over by Aeneas Junior, and in 1835 it was established in London. English and Scottish distillers use the Coffey still extensively. Aeneas Coffey Senior died in 1850 and his distillery in London was made over by his descendants to the foreman in 1872. On its website this firm (John Dore & Co. Ltd) says that it:

> … is the oldest distillery engineering business in the world. It is the successor company to Aeneas Coffey & Sons, established in Dublin, Ireland in 1830 and in London, England, UK in January 1835.[44]

Later the 'Railway Works' of the Dublin & South Eastern Railway were established at the site where Coffey's distillery had been, at the south-eastern end of Grand Canal Dock, between the Dock and Barrow Street. The office and mess of the locomotive staff, originally the only part of the works north of the railway, survived longest and could be still seen from Grand Canal Dock Station in the first years of the twenty-first century, though it had been greatly damaged by fire.

Now disappeared, the site today is occupied by Google's Montevetro building, the construction of which commenced in 2008.

Burnt-out office/mess of the locomotive staff of the Dublin & South Eastern Railway from Grand Canal Dock Station, 2006.

As far as professions are concerned, apart from provision merchants, dairy men, grocers, spirit dealers, vintners and tailors, *Thom's Directory* for 1868 lists two ropemakers; one rope, twine and net manufacturer; two sailmakers; one salt merchant; seven shipwrights, ship builders or boatbuilders (not counting the Dockyard Company and the Ringsend Foundry) and five car owners. Surprisingly only one person gave his profession as fisherman. There also was an artist.

In later years more modern industry branches moved to Ringsend. Pembroke Township (like Rathmines and Rathgar Township) had its own electricity generating stations since the 1890s to show their independence from Dublin City, which had firms producing electricity for lighting since 1880. The Pembroke 'Electric Lighting & Refuse Destructor Works' are shown on the 1907 OS map on South Lotts Road where Sportsco (formerly the ESB sport complex) is now. Those stations were taken over by the Electricty Supply Board (ESB) in 1929 even before Pembroke Urban District was incorporated into Dublin City.

The last foundry to operate in Ringsend was Hammond Lane Foundry. The firm is still in the area, and since 1898 has become one of the biggest metal recycling works in Ireland, but there is no foundry anymore. Evidence of this famous foundry can still be found on lamp posts and manhole covers in the area.

Another firm, James Beckett Ltd, which was well known in the building trade, was based in Ringsend for decades. Apart from early office blocks they built many of the houses in the South Lotts area of Ringsend. The most famous member of that family had nothing to do with building, though, and apart from his grandfather and uncles he had no real connection with Ringsend. One of the founders of the firm as well as his son lived for some time in neighbouring Sandymount.

Into modern times Ringsend was the village with the largest industrial sector among the four coastal villages of Dublin, as is shown by some advertisements of earlier years.

The Official Industrial Directory for Ireland in 1955 listed all manufacturing firms in Ireland that had reported back to them in the year 1954. Eighteen of the twenty-four firms listed in the area of the four coastal villages of Dublin 4 were in Ringsend, two in Irishtown and four in Sandymount. The following

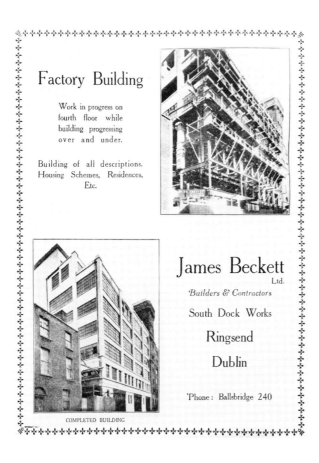

Advertisement, 1931.

Advertisements
from the Industrial
Directory 1955.

firms were mentioned for Ringsend (the category is given in brackets and
further information, if available, is in italics):

**Beckett, James, Ltd, South Dock Works, Ringsend (Builders/Contractors/
Joinery).** – *According to an advertisement in the Official Handbook of
Dublin 1930 the firm was established in 1845, which is highly unlikely as
James Beckett was only born around 1841. Other sources give 1870 as
the year the firm was established. This firm originally was a partnership
between the brothers James and William Becket. The partnership was
dissolved in the 1890s and from then on the firm traded as James Beckett
Ltd. One of the bigger projects of this firm was the building of the W.
and R. Jacobs Biscuits complex in Bishop Street. They are not in business
anymore.*

Boland's Mill, Grand Canal St and Ringsend Rd (Wheaten flour/Wheaten meal/Self-raising flour/Bread and flour confectionery/Animal compound feeding stuffs/Bran and Pollard). – *This mill was in existence in the 1830s. In 1873 the Pim brothers sold it to Patrick Boland. The mill stopped production in 2001. In 2016 work began to develop the older buildings, keeping their facades, but changing the insides into offices, apartments and hotels. The concrete corn silos that were much younger than the old mill buildings, were taken down.*

Bovril (Eire), 20, Ringsend Rd (Meat extract and cubes). – *The parent firm's seat is in the UK since 1889 and still producing there. Bovril is now owned by Unilever UK.*

Brunswick Sawmills Co. Ltd, South Dock Works, Ringsend Road (Sawmilling/Joinery/Floorings, Sheetings, Shelvings).

Counihan, E.A. & Sons Ltd, 3 Upper Grand Canal Street (Canned meats).

Counihan, Richards & Co. Ltd, Upper Grand Canal Street (Margarine).

Dock Milling Company Ltd, 38–43 Barrow Street (Wheaten flour/Animal compound feeding stuffs/Bran and pollard/Corn (oats, barley etc.). *The Dock Mill is shown on the 1837 OS map, just south of a smaller complex of buildings called Dock Chemical Works. Dock Mill only stopped working in the last quarter of the twentieth century; the building exists still with the same name, but now houses offices.*

Gerard's Ltd, Talisman Works, 48–50 Barrow Street (Marking inks/Soaps and detergents/Laundry press pads/Laundry and dyer's net bags).

Hull, Alexander & Co., Ltd, Ringsend Road (Joinery).

Irish Products, Ltd, Hibernian Works, Ringsend (Sausage casings/Tripe/Fats, edible/Animal compound feeding stuffs/Meat, blood, bone and liver meal/Fats, inedible). – *Thom's Commercial Directory for 1979 still listed the firm under the same address as 'Processors Animal By-Products'.*

Martin, H. & J. Ltd, 1–11 Upper Grand Canal Street (Joinery/Shop fittings (Showcases, counters, etc.) – wood/Concrete castings/Wooden stands).

Mining Co. of Ireland and Strachan Bros. Ltd, Ringsend Lead Works (Scrap Lead – smelting and refining of/Sheet Lead). – *The firm still exists, but now with an address in Clondalkin where they were set up in 1892.*

Mulholland, J. & Co., Dublin Rope Works, 99 Gordon Street, Ringsend (Ropes, twines and cords). *The firm was registered in 1919 under this name. The 1901 and 1911 censuses provide the following data: 1901: 'Joseph Mulholland, Roman Catholic, born in Dundalk, 52 years old, rope manufacturer, Teresa Mulholland, wife, Roman Catholic, born in Belfast, 52 years old.' They lived in South Lots Road with two daughters and two sons: son John Charles, born in Dublin, 36 years old, rope maker, and son William Joseph, born in Dublin, 21 years old, rope maker. According to the 1911 census the Mulholland family lived in South Lotts Road, Joseph now 71 years of age and his wife Teresa 68 years. Both daughters are still living at home, as well as son William Joseph, now 36 years old and giving 'rope works' as occupation. Joseph Mulholland gives his occupation as Rope Manufacturer and Shop Keeper.*

Richardsons (Dublin), Ltd, 49–50 Barrow St (Polishes, various/Furniture polish/Insecticides/ Desinfectants/Liquid Soap).

Ringsend Dockyard (Dublin) Ltd, Grand Canal Basin (General Engineering Works/Structural Steel and Iron Works/Shipbuilding and Repairing/ Various Parts for Ships and Boats (Metal)). – *The firm was also known as McMullan's after its director and main ship builder who lived in Leahy's Terrace at the border between Irishtown and Sandymount. The firm was in business from 1913 to 1963 and built many barges for the Grand Canal Company.*

Ryan, William P. Ltd, 52 Thorncastle St, Ringsend (Motor cars (assembly)/ Motor bodies – van and lorry/Omnibus bodies/Horse boxes/Motor vehicle upholstery). *The firm still sold cars in 1977.*[45]

Serck (Eire) Ltd, Cambridge Rd, Ringsend (Radiator Cores/Tanks (Various)/ Petrol Tanks (Road)). –*The firm later changed its name to Serck (Ireland) limited. It does not exist anymore.*

The major businesses in Ringsend today are no longer in manufacturing. The area around Grand Canal Dock is now sometimes referred to as 'Silicon Dock', as it houses international IT firms like Google, Facebook and Twitter.

More and more office blocks are being built in this area, accommodating firms in the service sector, such as large law and accountancy firms. The influx of so many new people working in the area has caused a change in the local infrastructure. More and more cafés are appearing, as well as sandwich shops, shops for take-away meals and specialised food shops, including a very good baker/confectioner just across MacMahon Bridge in Dublin 2.

Barrow Street houses the Dublin Sanitary Disposal Ltd headquarters. Ringsend Depot of Dublin Bus is not far away, situated on Ringsend Road, where the tram power station used to be. Part of Pigeon House Road is on the South Wall, while other parts are on the Poolbeg Peninsula and described with Irishtown. Firms that have Pigeon House Road as an address could be in either of the two villages. Under Ringsend should be mentioned Pigeon House Electricity Works; a waste removal firm; Hammond Lane, the former foundry and now scrap iron and metal firm and a firm of analytical laboratories. The latter is housed in a building of the old Pigeon House Hospital, near the sewage works. They are mainly involved in water and microbiological analyses.

EDUCATION

The two national schools in Ringsend are St Patrick's Boys National School and St Patrick's Girls National School, which are situated side by side and share the same premises on Cambridge Road. They are well regarded, as in 2009 a report of the Department of Education and Skills mentioned about the boys' school:

> The teachers are dedicated, committed and very competent.
> The overall quality of teaching is very good.
> The school atmosphere is positive, friendly and welcoming.
> Pupil behaviour is very good and respectful relations are fostered between pupils and staff.
> Local history is given very good attention in the school.[46]

As the schools co-operate, the report for the girls' school most likely was similar. Both schools stress Gaelic games in their sport curriculum.

As far as secondary schools are concerned, Ringsend does not have a secondary school in the traditional sense, but to improve Ringsend and give its inhabitants a better grounded education George Robert Charles Herbert,

Thirteenth Earl of Pembroke, founded the Pembroke Technical and Ringsend Fishery Schools in 1892. He was the elder son of Sidney Herbert, First Baron of Lea, the man who developed most of this area.

The school was later run by Pembroke Township and in the early 1920s already included some very modern classes.

> At Ringsend, the Pembroke Technical Instruction Committee have organized in a building originally designed as a School of Navigation, a technical school with a Day Trades' Preparatory department. It may be noted in connection with this school that it includes a very successful department for the teaching of motor engineering.[47]

With the incorporation of Pembroke Urban District into Dublin in 1930 the school was taken over by the City of Dublin Vocational Education Committee (CDVEC) which is now known as the City of Dublin Education and Training Board (CDETB). In the 1950s the school occupied the old Pembroke Town Hall at the corner of Merrion Road and Anglesea Road in Ballsbridge, but in 1982 a new building was erected on the corner of Cambridge Street and York Street which was called the Ringsend Technical Institute, known as Ringsend College or locally just as 'The Tech'. This second level school was built on the site of the original Pembroke Technical and Ringsend Fishery Schools.

One of the first governors of the Pembroke Technical and Ringsend Fishery School was William Frank Beckett, who had become a Commissioner of Pembroke Township in 1892. He was the father of the writer and Nobel Prize winner Samuel Beckett.

Ringsend College has diversified a lot since the time when it was a technical school. Now it is a fully-developed second level school which, 'respects that all students have different goals and abilities. Ringsend College sees it as its objective to help students to find, recognise and develop their talents in whatever field that may be.'[48]

In Further Education Courses Ringsend College combines IT skills, including software development, with business administration and horticulture. On top of that the college offers night classes in a wide range of subjects, including different aspects of household management, dressmaking, Spanish, pilates and yoga. Following the intentions of its founder and later the Pembroke Technical Instruction Committee, they still offer courses in marine engine maintenance as well as motorcar maintenance.

CHURCH TRADITIONS

Despite its name the church called 'Royal Chapel of St Matthew's Ringsend' is not situated in Ringsend but in Irishtown. Ringsend still has or had its own churches, though. St Patrick's Catholic Church of Ringsend first was built in 1858 as a chapel of ease for St Mary's, Haddington Road, which was then the parish church. In May 1881 Ringsend was separated from Haddington Road parish and united with the parish of Sandymount, which had been established in 1876. In 1905 finally Ringsend became a parish in its own right.[49]

The building of St Patrick's church as it stands now was erected in 1912. A view of this church from across the Grand Canal Basin still gives quite a maritime impression.

Funerals of Ringsend people often include the custom of carrying the coffin by relatives or friends across the bridge before entering the church. This tradition is well known and car drivers crossing the bridge will respect it, even if it means delays for them.

Formerly there was another building between the church and the River Dodder, which can be seen on the way up to Ringsend Bridge as bricked-up

Wall on the way to Ringsend Bridge.

Statue of Our Lady behind St Patrick's Church.

doors and a bricked-up window can be clearly made out in the wall. The 1907 OS map shows a building at this spot and so does the 1837 OS map, but that was before the church was built.

There are no buildings now behind that wall, but a bit further, just behind the big west window of the church a statue of Our Lady was erected in a little garden.

St Patrick's looks like any other neo-gothic church, with the entrance at one end and the altar at the other. The way it had to be built, however, caused the entrance to be built on the east and the altar on the west end – contrary to usual church building traditions. The tower also is not over the crossing as in old Romanesque and early Gothic churches. Ringsend church has its tower and steeple built up from the north-eastern corner, between nave and transept.

The church has a big stained glass window over the altar, designed by the Irish firm Earley & Co. and installed in 1939.

In a side chapel there is also a stained glass window of the Harry Clarke studios, designed by Harry Clarke and restored in 2016.

West window
of St Patrick's,
Ringsend.

Samuel Lewis mentions a 'place of worship for Wesleyan Methodists' in
Ringsend. The 1837 OS map shows this on the east side of Irishtown Road
opposite the southern end of Fitzwilliam Street. This Wesleyan Methodist
Chapel in Ringsend is also mentioned in a description in 1848.[50] This chapel
has long disappeared. The architect George Frances Beckett, a member
of the well-known family of architects and builders, erected a Methodist
Church in 1904 at the corner of what then was Riverview Avenue and
now is Dermot O'Hurley Avenue, just north of the border to Irishtown.
This church has been demolished, as has the Sandymount Presbyterian
Church. Both congregations now worship together with the Sandymount
Methodist congregation in Christ Church, Sandymount. The site of the
former Methodist Church in Ringsend is now occupied by the Summerhill
Apartment Block.

The former Ringsend Mission Hall and YMCA in York Road is hardly known outside Ringsend. York Road is at the edge of Ringsend village and runs parallel to the road from the East Link Bridge. The Mission Hall can be seen from that road right in the middle, between the bridge and the toll station, but few car drivers dare to look around when driving on narrow and bumpy York Road or on the heavily-trafficked road leading to the toll bridge. The hall was built in 1896 by two unmarried daughters of Victor Bewley (of Bewley's Café) who were strong supporters of the YMCA movement. In the 1990s it was planned to demolish the hall to make way for apartments. This, however, was not possible as the two Bewley ladies had insisted in their last will that it had to be kept in perpetuity. For several years now the charitable Anchorage Project runs its Fair Play Café, playschool and adjoining garden centre there, with the profit going to communities in need in Ireland as well as in other countries.

During the last decade Ringsend has been changed to the extent that instead of being looked down on by 'richer' villages as in earlier times, it now is a very desirable address, with modern apartment buildings near the water (Grand Canal Dock, Dodder and Liffey), not far from the city centre and readily accessible by bus and DART.

ART DECO

Ringsend has some good examples of Art Deco buildings. A late example of that style is the Public Library, situated between Fitzwilliam Street and what now is called St Patrick's Villas. Originally St Patrick's Villas was just a terrace of houses on a street called Thomas Street, which after the incorporation of Pembroke Township into Dublin City was referred to as Thomas Street East, to differentiate it from Thomas Street West between Cornmarket and St James's Gate in Dublin 8. Thomas Street as a street name has completely disappeared in Ringsend and the street is only known as St Patrick's Villas.

Ringsend Library was erected in 1937 on a little oblong between Bridge Street, Fitzwilliam Street and St Patrick's Villas (Thomas Street), with its entrance facing the latter. This oblong seems to have been cleared for the library as both the 1837 and the 1907 OS maps show houses where the plaza around Ringsend Library is now.

The little plaza beside it has a sculpture by local sculptor Joe Moran showing a partly open door, a memorial for women who became victims of domestic abuse.

The former tram
power station.

Fitzwilliam Street houses another Art Deco building that is slightly more difficult to find, even though it is not far from the library. It was built in 1925 as a cinema, originally called 'Rinn' but later changed to Regal. This cinema opened on 29 November 1925, just in time for the Christmas season. It ceased operating as a cinema on 10 January 1965.

The architect of the cinema, Thomas Francis McNamara (1867–1947), worked as a church architect at the beginning of his career, but was later involved in designing other buildings. In the Pembroke area he built the Bridge Building in Upper Baggot Street, as well as cottages and houses in the Bath Avenue area in the early 1920s. He lived in the neighbourhood and quite a few houses in the Pembroke Urban District are listed as his work in the *Dictionary of Irish Architects*.[51] His addresses included 36 Belmont Avenue in Donnybrook, 67 Northumberland Road in Ballsbridge and for the last twenty years of his life 'Fairy Villa', Sandymount Avenue, at the corner with Merrion Road in Ballsbridge. It was T.F. McNamara who advised Harry Clarke to take up art instead of studying architecture.

From 1986 to 2009 the former cinema was used by FÁS (Foras Áiseanna Saothair) for training courses. Since December 2013 it has housed the Pentecostal Church called Amazing Grace, which had to leave its former premises in Irishtown.[52]

Ringsend Road has another Art Deco building between the Dodder and the Grand Canal. This used to be a tram power station. When the trams disappeared it took on a new lease of life as a music studio.

GRAND CANAL DOCK AND SURROUNDINGS

There are many mills at Grand Canal Dock, of which Boland's Mill and Dock Mill are the best known. In 2000 Grand Canal Dock looked still very much the way it had looked 100 years earlier, with warehouses and mills lining it, even though new apartment blocks had already appeared on one side of it.

Three years later a building had been erected in the docks. It is the Interpretative Centre of Irish Waterways. Because of its shape and situation it was immediately dubbed 'The Box in the Docks'. Since 2003, when this photo was taken, big steel and glass office and apartment blocks have been erected, now dwarfing most of the old mills and warehouses. Those of the old mills that have survived the so-called Celtic Tiger times have been turned into offices and are squeezed in between huge newly-built office blocks.

Some of the old mills still show their names, which are difficult to read as there are no open spaces and the thoroughfares between the buildings are narrow.

Grand Canal Dock, 2003, with old mills and warehouses on the Ringsend side.

Dock Mill has now been turned into offices.

Dock Mill was in business even in the second half of the twentieth century, but by now it has been turned into an office block and the name on the gable is obscured by the erection of fire escape stairs on the outside of the building.

Boland's Flour Mill was built in stone in the early nineteenth century and later dwarfed by four huge concrete silos built in the 1940s. It is only 'Boland's Mill' since 1873 when Patrick Boland bought it from the brothers Pim who ran it before him. The mill stopped working in 2001 and the buildings stood empty for several years. In 2015 Dublin City Council approved a plan to develop the area, maintaining the facades of the buildings from the 1830s and the 1870s. The plan includes offices, apartments, shops, cafés, restaurants and an exhibition building. The development work started with the removal of the domineering but rather ugly looking concrete silos of the 1950s. Demolishing them took 242 days of work and was completed in July 2016. The re-development of the area, which will be called Boland's Quay, is scheduled to be finished in 2018.

Boland's Mill's connection with the Easter Rising of 1916 is that it was held by Éamon de Valera, together with Boland's Biscuit Bakery at the corner

Part of Boland's Mill, with the concrete silos still in existence, 2013.

Grand Canal Basin from Grand Canal Dock Station, 2006.

of Grand Canal Street and Macken Street (at that stage still called Great Clarence Street) in Dublin 2, a building that despite its connection with the Easter Rising has long been demolished to make room for the Treasury Building.

The ensemble of buildings of the former Boland's Mill looked completely different after the big concrete silos were taken down during 2016.

Some years ago this area was for a long time one of the playgrounds of the so-called Celtic Tiger era, with its favourite toys – building cranes – in evidence, creating a radically different streetscape.

MacMahon Bridge was named after Dublin born Seán MacMahon (1893–1955), who fought under Éamon de Valera in 1916 and later became Quartermaster General of the Irish Republican Army. The bridge replaced the older Victoria Bridge, which itself had replaced its forerunner, the Brunswick Bascule. Like its two predecessors, the old MacMahon Bridge was a drawbridge. During the last years of its existence it had not been opened, but part of the apparatus to open it could still be seen in 2005.

Grand Canal Dock, 2011.

Victoria Bridge was not only used by cars but also by the tram lines Numbers 1, 2 and 3 going to Ringsend and Sandymount. One day a very rare traffic accident occurred: a collision between a ship and a tram.

> Ringsend Road, Dublin, Cymric of Beaumorris ran into Victoria drawbridge and spiked a tram number 233. A window was broken but there were no injuries.[53]

This was not the only 'dispute' between a ship and this bridge as another newspaper reported:

> This story will probably afford great relief to countless Sandymount civil servants because it substantiates in toto the excuses made by them for arriving late at their respective offices yesterday. But if having read it some higher executive officer is still somewhat doubtful, just refer him to the solitary *Irish Times* reporter, who, with countless other workers and shop assistants sat for half an hour while the crew of a three masted Arklow

sailing vessel battled to clear its bowsprit from the railings of nearby Victoria bridge. Yes it was the Happy Harry en route from Waterford to Dublin that caused the trouble. For years she had docilely glided through the open gates of the swing bridge on the main Ringsend thoroughfare to her berth in the Grand Canal basin. But yesterday, for some perverse reason she missed the opening, rammed her bowsprit into the railings of one of the open gate wings and in matter of seconds had completely disorganised the rush hour traffic streaming citywards. The hour was 8.50 a.m. with every bus packed to capacity.[54]

The new MacMahon Bridge cannot be opened and the boats crossing under it in general do not carry sail.

Gordon Street 2011 with the apartment block in the former gasometer in the background.

The building activity did not stop at the banks of the Grand Canal, but spread to both sides of the canal basin and even the South Lotts were affected, with their little houses ducking under cranes and the resulting huge new structures.

The cranes are gone; the little houses are still there, most of them nowadays with an extension in the back and the roof converted to get an additional room in the attic. From a viewpoint that hides the tall new blocks the area still has its own charm.

The area of 'South Lotts' was developed by the builder and contractor firm James Beckett in the three decades between 1890 and 1920. The terraced houses are small, some with only one and others with two stories, most with only a small patio in the back and none with a front garden. Many of them have been bought and renovated lately.

Not far away behind the little houses another interesting structure remains from Ringsend's industrial times: the old gasometer. This gasometer or 'gas holder' was of the telescopic type, which means that it expanded or contracted, depending on the amount of gas inside it. The sketch explains the principle.

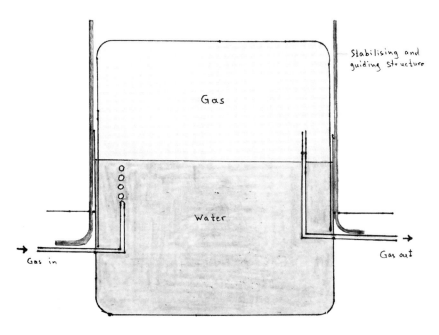

The principle of a telescopic gas holder.

'The Alliance' apartment block in the former gasometer.

The inner court of 'The Alliance'.

The upper dome rose when gas was pumped in. As the height could be considerable, it had to be kept straight. The Ringsend gas holder was column-guided, which meant that it had an external steel 'skeleton' to keep it in place. Gas holders of this type were common in Victorian times. When no longer in use the gas holder was dismantled, but the outside skeleton was made into a protected structure and remained.

Inside this structure an apartment block was built and the complex is officially called *The Alliance*, but it is often still referred to as the Gasometer. Its circular structure must make the plan of each apartment slightly unusual.

'Google Bridge' across Barrow Street, looking west.

Inside the complex a circular yard picks up the shape of the block and ensures that the apartments get light from both sides.

The area between the former Gasometer and Grand Canal Dock has been completely renewed with new office blocks. Google, which occupies a number of those blocks on both sides of Barrow Street, has built a first-floor connection between three of its buildings on different sides of Barrow Street. Google Bridge stretches between Google Docks on the west side of Barrow Street and both Gordon House and Gasworks House on the east side.

Despite all the modern development, Ringsend is still rather green, though most of the gardens cannot be seen from the streets. A view from the rooftop

Ringsend from above.

of a big hotel on the city side of Grand Canal Dock shows an astonishing amount of trees.

SPORT

Ringsend was known for its rowing clubs since the first half of the nineteenth century, but its connection with sport is much older. More than 350 years ago a sporting event was reported in *The Intelligencer* on 15 May 1665:

> We have here upon the Strand several races; but the most remarkable was
> by the Ringsend Coaches (Which is an odde kind of carre, and generally

used in the countrye). There were a matter of twenty-five of them, and His
Excellency the Lord Deputy bestowed a piece of plate upon him that won
the race, and the second, third and fourth were rewarded with money. It is
a new institution, and likely to become an annual custom; For the humour
of it gives much satisfaction, there being at least 5,000 spectators.

The Lord Deputy mentioned in this report was Thomas Butler, Sixth Earl
of Ossory, who stood in as deputy for his father, James Butler, First Duke of
Ormonde, the Lord Lieutenant of that time.

Apart from this race, the earliest sports organisations in Ringsend date
from 1836 when a rowing club was formed, soon followed by others on the
Ringsend shore of the River Dodder. During the next decades those clubs
found the location less than ideal, mainly because of the industrialisation
which led to even more pollution in a river which was more or less used as
a sewer. Eventually all rowing clubs moved to Islandbridge on the Liffey,
west of Dublin city. Coastal rowing, however, stayed in Ringsend. The East
Coast Rowing Council, formed in 1936, still has two clubs in Ringsend
– St Patrick's Rowing Club and Stella Maris Rowing Club. Their boats
are built like the former hobblers' boats and this way they keep an old
tradition alive.

In 1909 Ringsend Park was handed over by the Pembroke Estate to
Pembroke Urban Council, which from the beginning developed grounds for
sports there. The different pitches now are used by several soccer clubs, quite
a few of them based in Ringsend, and by Clanna Gael Fontenoy GAA club.
As far as team sports are concerned, Ringsend, like many other working class
areas, has a great interest in soccer. One of the oldest soccer clubs in Dublin,
Liffey Wanderers, has a close connection with Ringsend. There are also
Cambridge Boys, Markievicz Celtic, Pearse Rangers, Ringsend Rovers and
St Patrick's CYFC. South Dock Celtic FC only survived for some years, but
Shamrock Rovers, which were founded in Ringsend, are still going strong,
though not in Ringsend. Shelbourne FC was founded in the Beggars' Bush/
Irishtown area, but they played for many years in Ringsend in the stadium
that still is named after them.

South Lotts is a part of Ringsend that from the time this part of land was
reclaimed from the sea was regarded as part of Ringsend, even though it
belonged to the Parish of St Mark on Grand Brunswick Street (now Pearse
Street) and not to St Matthew's as the rest of the village did. Not far from
Ringsend Park, on the South Lotts side of the Dodder and directly beside
the river, Ringsend has its own stadium, built for a soccer club whose name
it still bears, but is now exclusively used for greyhound racing.

Shelbourne Park Stadium, seen from Fitzwilliam Quay.

Shelbourne Park Stadium was named after Shelbourne FC who built it and played there from 1913 to 1955. Greyhound races started in the stadium in 1927 and are still going on there. At some time in the second half of the twentieth century the stadium saw speedway races as well.

Adjacent to Shelbourne Park to the south on South Lotts Road, is ESB Sportsco Leisure Centre with possibilities for soccer, tennis, squash, table tennis, swimming and yoga. It also includes a fitness centre, a café, an aerobic studio, and a physiotherapy clinic.

During the last few years Grand Canal Dock was discovered for water sport. It now has a windsurfing school offering kayak classes, and there is also a cable wakeboard park.

RINGSEND ADDRESSES

Like all the other villages, Ringsend has addresses that are well known even outside that village. The best known name goes back to an address that does not exist anymore: Shamrock Rovers FC was 'born' in this area and took its name from Shamrock Avenue, a tiny thoroughfare parallel to Irishtown Road (in the Ringsend part), connecting Fairview Avenue and Fairview, an area that now is called The Square.

Other addresses were less glorious like Rum Row or Whiskey Row, which appeared in Griffith's Valuation in 1848, both containing rather dilapidated houses. According to this source all twelve families living in Whiskey Row had the same landlord. Rum Row was shorter, with only three family names appearing, of which two seem to have been subtenants of the third who was a tenant himself. Those rows ran between Thorncastle Street and the Dodder. Rum Row disappeared rather early, while Whiskey Row survived for some time. It was at some stage renamed 'Dodder Place' and appears as such on the 1907 OS map. Later it was replaced by the apartment blocks of Whelan House and O'Rahilly House.

Further east in Ringsend, situated between Rope Walk Place and Caroline Row was a short street that originally must have been a very good address, as it was called Quality Row. It did not keep its quality, though, and after the 1870s, with more and more tenements appearing, the name became disused. On the 1907 map it is called Parkview Place, the name it still has today. Now that Grand Canal Dock has morphed into Silicon Dock, the whole area of the South Lotts as well as Charlotte Quay are top addresses in the area.

PEOPLE FROM AND IN RINGSEND

Murphy is a very common name in Ringsend and as the same first names tend to appear in the same family, there had to be other distinctions. In one family of Murphys one finds names like William Craneman Murphy, William Boxer Murphy and John Butcher Murphy to distinguish family members from others with the same name.[55]

Another Murphy family from Ringsend soon moved away from there. The first one of note was Michael Murphy, a coal merchant and importer. His son J.P. Murphy was a shipping agent and coal factor who, in the 1840s, lived at 27 Great Brunswick (now Pearse) Street for some time before moving to 17 Eden Quay. This family became involved in the shipping companies Palgrave Murphy & Company Ltd, Michael Murphy Ltd and Dublin Steamship Ltd, which they owned, or at least part-owned. These companies were later absorbed into other shipping lines like the British and Irish Steam Packet Company (B&I). For some time a Murphy of that same family was one of B&I's directors. Some members of the family were knighted, but at that stage they had left Ringsend. Having become rich they had moved to areas like Blackrock, Shrewsbury Road and Merrion Square.[56]

Ringsend has mainly been a workers' area and when someone from there became rich and famous like the 'Shipping Murphys' they usually moved out. There is one, however, for whom it is right and fitting that he should be connected with a workers' area: when James Connolly returned to Ireland from America in 1910, he lived for some time in South Lotts Road.[57]

Whelan House, which replaced Dodder Place, was named after Patrick Whelan, an active Gaelic Leaguer from Ringsend who was killed on the railway line near Boland's Mill in 1916.

Ringsend received some mentions in literature. Oliver St John Gogerty's poem with the starting line 'I will live in Ringsend' might be known though it does not describe the standard type of citizen living in this village nowadays. A lesser-known anecdote which concerns Brendan Behan was reported by Benedict Kiely, who described Behan accompanying a friend who had married into a Ringsend family. They met the in-laws of this friend in a Ringsend pub and got into a dispute. They seem to have lost the dispute and not only with words as they were compelled to:

> ... wade to safety across the limitless strand of Sandymount where the tide was running but fortunately not near the full. Next day Brendan, disguised in bruises and sticking-plaster, said to me, in simple explanation: 'They're a peculiar crowd of savages in Ringsend.'[58]

In defence of the people of Ringsend it has to be said that Brendan Behan was no saint himself, especially after taking a drink, and he never took just one.

3

IRISHTOWN

When people talk about Ringsend, they often include Irishtown. The Hibernian Marine School, for instance, sometimes is reported as having been founded in Ringsend. Earlier references disagree: Richard Lewis mentions a marine nursery that was founded in 1766 and later became the Hibernian Marine School:

> And for that purpose a voluntary subscription was raised, by which the Society, in 1766, were enabled to open a house at Irish-Town, near Ringsend, for the reception of twenty boys, and as the subscriptions and benefactions encreased, they enlarged the number to fifty, afterwards to sixty, and gradually more, as their fund enabled them.[1]

The school grew rapidly and only two years later in 1768 the governors bought a plot at Sir John Rogerson's Quay where they erected a purpose-built school into which the boys moved in 1773. This is the building shown by Malton in his prints of Dublin. Later the school moved across the river to Clontarf, where in 1968 it amalgamated with Mountjoy School to become Mountjoy & Marine School. This in 1972 amalgamated further with Bertrand & Rutland School to become Mount Temple Comprehensive School, which always had a strong interest in music. Four pupils of this school formed a rock band in 1976 – called U2.

It does not happen often that the existence of Irishtown as a unit in its own right is acknowledged. Most old Irish maps mention Ringsend, Merrion, Booterstown and Blackrock along the coast going south from the Liffey. Irishtown is mentioned less often in older maps and hardly ever in modern ones, except in a map of Leinster attached to a description of Leinster in a 1922 series by the Cambridge University Press. This map is in the unusual

scale of one inch to 12.5 miles, which is in modern terms in the scale of
1:793,750. This map does not mention Ringsend on the coast south of
Dublin between the mouth of the Liffey and Dún Laoghaire (on the map still
called Kingstown), but instead from north to south Irish T[n], Booterstown,
Blackrock and Salt Hill are marked.[2]

SOME HISTORY OF IRISHTOWN

Richard Lewis's guide shows that in the second half of the eighteenth century
Ringsend and Irishtown were regarded as two distinct villages. This is also
shown in historic maps.

On this map north is on the left. It shows that both Ringsend and Irishtown
are situated on a raised ridge, as the parts east and west of the villages (top
and bottom of the illustration) are described as 'Part of the Strand'. This
ridge was high enough to keep both villages above the high water mark,
except in especially high tides. The darker grey rectangle at the south end of
Irishtown (right on the map) is St Matthew's Church with its graveyard to
the south. East of Irishtown a wall seems to enclose 'My Lord's Pond' and
the buildings reaching across this pond to the wall at the edge of the strand
might be Murphy's Baths or their forerunners. The 1837 OS map shows
Murphy's Baths on this spot.

As far as the name of Irishtown is concerned, there are several explanations.
J.W. de Courcy is of the opinion that the origin of the name is obscure
and that it might have arisen during the Reformation.[3] This is unlikely as

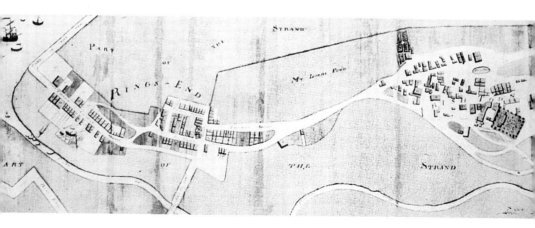

Ringsend and Irishtown by Jonathan Barker 1762.

the antagonism between the ruling Anglo-Irish classes and the native Irish did not start with the Reformation, neither in Dublin nor in other places that have suburbs called 'Irishtown'. Bennett[4] mentions a decree of Dublin Corporation decades before the Reformation. In the year 1454 it was ordered that: '… all men and women of Irish blood whether nuns, clerics, journeymen apprentices, servants or beggars to vacate the city within four weeks …'

Dublin Corporation then was run by merchants and guild members with English roots, the majority of them from Bristol. For these people the Irish were suspect, especially considering the attacks of the 'Wild Irish' from the Wicklow Mountains that occasionally devastated the hinterland of the city. The professions for Irish people mentioned in this decree give an interesting insight into an early class system. Even though there obviously were apprentices and journeymen of Irish blood, there were no masters. As far as servants were concerned, at least in later centuries Irish servants were allowed into the city during the day, but they had to leave at dusk and walk to their homes, which by decree should be at least two miles away from the city.

There are other places called 'Irishtown' near Dublin as well as near other towns of the Pale. A modern list gives four townlands with the name of Irishtown in the county of Dublin alone. Altogether there are at least twenty-one townlands in Ireland called 'Irishtown' of which nineteen are in the province of Leinster. Of the four Irishtowns in County Dublin, the townland south-east of Ringsend is the smallest, with an area of 56 acres, while the one in Palmerston parish is the biggest, with an area of 260 acres.

According to de Courcy this coastal Irishtown had more inhabitants than Ringsend in the mid-seventeenth century. Later censuses gave similar numbers for Ringsend and Irishtown, with the difference that the majority of the inhabitants in Ringsend were Protestants, whereas most inhabitants of Irishtown were Catholics.

CHURCHES

The oldest building in Irishtown is the church with the official name Royal Chapel of St Matthew's in Ringsend. As it was clearly built in Irishtown townland it is locally known as 'Irishtown Church'. The official name indicates that even at the beginning of the eighteenth century Ringsend and Irishtown were sometimes regarded as one unit, something with which the real Irishtown people did not and still do not agree. The designation 'Ringsend' for St Matthew's probably is connected with the fact that it was the residents of Ringsend that wanted their own church, as John D'Alton reports in his entry 'Ringsend':

> In 1703, the inhabitants of this place having become numerous by the accession of many officers of the port, seamen and strangers, and being not only distant from Donnybrook, their parish church, but prevented from resorting thither by tides and waters overflowing the highway, an act was passed authorizing Viscount Merrion to convey any quantity of land, not exceeding two acres for a church and churchyard for their accommodation, and the Archbishop of Dublin was empowered to apply £100 out of the forfeited tithes towards building same, and endowment which afterwards took effect in the adjacent village of Irishtown.[5]

The quotation also makes it clear, that D'Alton knew very well that the church was situated in Irishtown and not in Ringsend.

The Viscount Merrion mentioned by D'Alton was Thomas, Fourth Viscount Fitzwilliam of Merrion who died in 1704, the year in which the church was built.

Irishtown Church (Royal Chapel of St Matthew's Ringsend).

The entrance of St Matthew's with the foundation date of the church (1704) over the door.

The church tower was erected in 1713, nearly ten years after the church itself. Other than the church it was financed by Dublin Corporation, as it functioned as a landmark for sailors in Dublin Bay. At that time the sea came up to where Pembroke Street is now. Today after some renovations and enlargements, the tower is the oldest original part of the church, but still not as old as the date carved in stone above the door (1704) as this is the date for the building of the original church, not the building of the tower.

Like most of the churches of that time, it was rumoured to be a convenient place to hide contraband, either in the vaults under the nave or in the tower. The church was rebuilt in 1878–79 when a transept was added, with only the tower surviving of the older building.[6] Most likely the contraband, if any, had been sold before that time.

The windows over the communion table are quite dark. They were made and installed in the years 1886–92 by the Irish firm Earley & Powell. This probably was in connection with the enlargement and renovation of the church.

They show from left to right: Christ as Light of the World, Christ Calming the Storm; The Baptism of Christ, Supper at Emmaus; Christ as Good Shepherd and Christ with Mary and Martha.

Like many of the neo-Gothic churches of the eighteenth and nineteenth centuries, the church has a wooden roof, which shows superior craftsmanship in the timberwork in the crossing.

St Matthew's, which had been a chapel of ease for St Mary's, Donnybrook, became a parish church in 1870 with Canon Robert Baker Stoney as the first rector.

The church stands in a little churchyard with some gravestones on the left of it, but with the main part to the right. The first Minister of St Matthew's, Reverend John Bouhéreau, was laid to rest there in 1726, as was the first Roman Catholic parish priest of the re-organised St Mary's parish of Donnybrook and Irishtown, Fr Peter Richard Clinch, in 1791. At that stage there were no Catholic graveyards, so the churchyards of the Church of Ireland were used for everybody, except in some cases where Huguenots and Jews had their own burial places in Dublin. One of the graves

Earley & Powell stained-glass windows in Irishtown church.

St Matthew's, roof in the crossing.

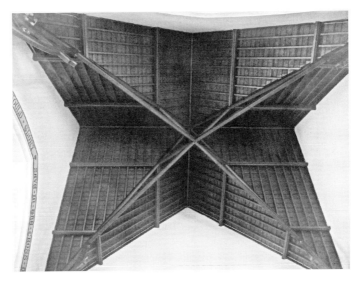

in Irishtown is that of the snuff manufacturer and tobacconist Lundy Foot, who was murdered in 1835 by one of his tenants. It is said that he was not a benevolent landlord – quite the contrary. Some of the Vavasour family are buried here also, as is Richard Cranfield of Cranfield's Baths. The last funeral in this churchyard was in 1872.

As in the other old graveyards in this area (Donnybrook and Merrion) headstones are not always situated in their original places and they often are badly weathered and covered with lichen, making them hard to read. In Irishtown Graveyard one gravestone of 1857 is still quite legible. If it is standing in its original place, the graveyard must have been enlarged, as this is one of the gravestones on the left (north) side of the church whereas the 1762 map only shows a graveyard on the right (south) side of the church.

Other churches used the former schoolhouse of the National Girls' School for Ringsend and Irishtown. From 1988 until July 2006 the Christian Brethren used the old girls' school, which then was known as 'Irishtown Gospel Hall'.

In April 2007 this building was reopened by the Metropolitan Church Dublin, a Pentecostal Church. From 2013 it has been used by the Abundant Grace Christian Assembly, another Pentecostal Church. The building, a protected structure, was owned by the National Asset Management Agency (NAMA) at that time. According to the Abundant Grace Christian Assembly their offer to buy the building was rejected by NAMA. Now they have secured the use of the former 'Regal' cinema in Ringsend. Lately the former school building was sold to a private developer.

Former girls' national school, Irishtown.

The first Roman Catholic chapel in Irishtown does not exist anymore. It had served as a parish church for a long time. It was possibly built in the seventeenth century, during the time of James II.[7] After 1787 when the parish of Irishtown, Donnybrook, Ringsend and Sandymount was separated from the parish of Booterstown, at least the first two parish priests of the new parish lived near the Chapel in Irishtown. According to the first OS map (1837 series) this chapel was situated at the corner of Pembroke Street and Chapel Avenue. D'Alton mentions that it had 'a particularly fine altar-piece'.[8]

Around the middle of the nineteenth century this chapel became structurally unsafe and it was decided to build a new church. This church was built further south, just barely north of the townland border between Irishtown and Sandymount and thus still officially in Irishtown. As it later became the parish church of the parish called Sandymount and as most parishioners do not realise that it is officially in Irishtown, it will be described in the Sandymount section.

SCHOOLS

The first school in Irishtown was built in 1832 and was situated on Church Avenue, south of the church, at the corner with Irishtown Road. The building is shown on the 1837 map but not described as a school. This became St Matthew's National School for Boys. The equivalent National School for Girls was built in 1904 by James Franklin Fuller (1835–1925), the same architect who also had been responsible for the rebuilding of St Matthew's in 1878–79 and who was considered an authority on the Hiberno-Romanesque style.[9]

After the building of new national schools for boys and girls, this building was no longer used as a schoolhouse and subsequently served several religious communities as their meeting hall.

National Girls' School Irishtown, c. 1910.

Former national school as seen from Irishtown Garda Station.

In 1959 the schools for boys and girls were merged and a new building was erected for St Matthew's National School in Cranfield Place on Irishtown townlands. This location is regarded as Irishtown by some people and as Sandymount by others. In 1969 St Stephen's School merged with it and the school was extended in 1985, 2001, 2010, 2011 and 2013.

GREENS AND MEMORIALS

Irishtown, like Sandymount, has a green. To be precise, Irishtown has more than one such green. The one usually referred to as Irishtown green is smaller than Sandymount Green. It has shops around it as has the Green in Sandymount.

This small Irishtown green has a monument, erected in 1894 for Dr William Ashford in grateful acknowledgment of his medical services to the community. Dr Ashford was the grandson of the painter William Ashford who lived in what is now Roslyn Park in Sandymount. The inscription on this monument reads:

Irishtown Green.

(front:)	*(back:)*
ERECTED	THE FOLLOWING
(illegible)	WERE
BY	THE COMMITTEE
PUBLIC SUBSCRIPTION	W. MENORY.
TO COMMEMORATE	J. CULLEN.
THE MEMORY OF	D. M^CGRATH.
DR. WM. ASHFORD	E. DOYLE.
FOR THE VALUABLE	W. CREESE.
SERVICE RENDERED	S. COONEY.
FOR A PERIOD OF	S. WEAFER.
HALF A CENTURY TO	P. M^CGRATH.
THE POOR OF	E. C. *(illegible)*
ST. MARY'S PARISH	

The four short stone pillars between the monument and the trees originally held a platform. The 1907 OS map shows this with the inscription 'Fire Escape Stand'. This fire escape was a ladder on wheels, used to rescue people from upper stories during a fire.

Another green area in Irishtown has occasionally been called 'the Green of Irishtown' – a strip of green strand from the end of Strand Street to Cranfield Place. The 1907 OS map marks this strip at the seashore as 'The Green'. It was known for centuries as a place for sport events and a cricket match played on it is mentioned in the *Universal Advertiser* in September 1757.[10]

This 'Green of Irishtown' is still there, though it is no longer directly beside the sea. There is a monument on this green as well – the Irish Mercantile Marine Memorial – erected for the members of the mercantile marine who lost their lives during the 'Emergency' as the Second World War is still called in Ireland. The memorial was unveiled in 1984 and is surrounded by trees selected to represent the names of the vessels that served the country at the time. Walter Kennedy[11] mentions all ships that visited Dublin port between 1939 and 1945. From his book can be learnt that the Dublin-based shipping line Irish Shipping Ltd named its ships after trees. Kennedy mentions *Irish Alder*, *Irish Ash*, *Irish Beech*, *Irish Cedar*, *Irish Elm*, *Irish Fir*, *Irish Hazel*, *Irish Larch*, *Irish Oak*, *Irish Pine*, *Irish Plane*, *Irish Poplar*, *Irish Rose*, *Irish Spruce* and *Irish Willow*. Some of the trees named have been planted around this memorial, for instance ash, poplar, spruce and pine, as well as beech, cedar, elm and oak.

Irish Mercantile Marine Memorial.

A naval connection is also maintained on the reclaimed land developed in the second half of the twentieth century. Some of the roads were named after ships. The *Kerlogue*, after which Kerlogue Road was named, saved many lives during the 'Emergency' years, when she was attacked from both sides. The *Cymric* of Cymric Road became famous through her accident with a No. 3 tram on Victoria Bridge in Ringsend in 1921. She sank in 1944, with the loss of eleven lives. The *City of Bremen* of Bremen Road, Bremen Avenue and Bremen Grove rescued thirty-three sailors of the Dutch ship *Amor* in 1940. In 1942 she was bombed in the Bay of Biscay and her crew were saved by the *Kerlogue*. The *Leukos* of Leukos Road was a trawler, built in 1914 and torpedoed in 1940 with the loss of eleven lives. The *Isolda* of Isolda

Road was a lightship tender. She was bombed in 1940 while heading out from Rosslare to re-supply nearby lightships with relief crews and Christmas provisions. Six of her crew died and seven were wounded. The *Clonlara* of Clonlara Road was torpedoed in 1941 with the loss of lives. The *Kyleclare* of Kyleclare Road was torpedoed by a German U-boat whose commander insisted he had not seen her neutral markings. Eighteen lives were lost. The *Irish Pine* of Pine Road was torpedoed on an Atlantic run with the loss of thirty-three men.[12]

Bigger than the Irishtown green in the centre of the village, this green spot with the above described memorial is a nice shady area near St Matthew's Church. Unluckily it is surrounded by a triangle of very busy roads: Beach Road, which carries traffic from the city centre via Ringsend to Dún Laoghaire; Church Avenue and Seán Moore Road which combine at the eastern end of the Green and lead towards the East Link toll bridge, the container harbour and the ferry port. Because of the traffic situation this green is not easily accessible.

One of the above-mentioned roads – Seán Moore Road – shows on its signs that Dublin City Council sticks with the custom of having the Irish name of a road on the top row. On the other hand their signmakers do not seem to have much knowledge about placing a síneadh fada, as one Irish version of the name on the road sign reads *Bóthar Sheán Uí Mhórdha*, wheras around the corner another sign gives the Irish name as *Bothar Sheain Ui Mhordha*.

There is another interesting memorial in Irishtown, something that a chance passer-by might wonder about. It is not far from the Irish Mercantile Marine Memorial and was once part of the Green of Irishtown.

The 1907 OS map shows this spot still directly beside the sea. The inscription 'Waxie's Dargle' on the stone will appear enigmatic for many. This refers to a custom of Dublin trade guilds, who used to drive out into the country on public holidays to a pleasant place at the banks of the River Dargle between Enniskerry and Bray, where each guild had its own place for a picnic. The Guild of Shoemakers and Cobblers (a trade whose members were called 'waxies', as they waxed the thread they used) were different, for the simple reason that there members did not have the money to drive so far out of town. Their 'Dargle' was a green spot on the strand of Irishtown. The stone commemorates this spot. Nearly opposite it is a street sign that proves that this area had been much nearer the sea before, as it says:

Radharc an Baighe
Bayview

The only bay you might be able to see from there today would be a parking bay.

People planning a day out would not think of Irishtown nowadays, but 200 years ago it looked very different. Sea bathing was en vogue and the strand of Irishtown was well known for Dublin citizens as a good place for a swim.

> A stranger, who should proceed along the entire coast from Ringsend, and through this place to Sandymount, in the summer months, and at a particular time of the tide, would not be a little struck with the swarm of naked figures presented to his view, enjoying the luxury of a sea-bath on the beautiful sands which margin this portion of the bay. On these occasions, almost the whole population of Dublin, he might suppose, were seized with this bathing-mania ... 20,000 people are estimated to bathe every tide in Dublin bay during the summer months, and many even continue the practice through the winter.[13]

Until the beginning of the nineteenth century it was rather normal that men bathed in the nude. There is still sea-bathing in Dublin Bay, even in winter, but the numbers are much lower now either on the Shelly Banks of Irishtown or the Half Moon Swimming Club on the South Wall in Ringsend (as well as beside the Seapoint Martello Tower and the Forty Foot in Sandycove) than they used to be 200 years ago. And swimming togs are required today, even at the Forty Foot.

IRISHTOWN GARDA STATION

The Gardaí occupy an important building at the south-eastern end of Irishtown. This is not the first police station in the area, but the third or possibly the fourth – all of them in Irishtown. The first that could be documented was built in 1831 at the corner of Irishtown Road and the aptly named Barrack Lane, as the building in question was built as barracks for the Dublin Metropolitan Police (DMP). It was not the most favoured posting for members of the DMP, possibly because Irishtown inhabitants were mainly working-class people who traditionally mistrusted the police.

> Throughout the nineteenth and early twentieth centuries there was fairly widespread hostility towards the DMP in the lower-class area of the capital.[14]

The former DMP barracks Irishtown.

In 1925 the Dublin Metropolitan Police was incorporated into the Garda Síochána. Later the Garda Síochána took over the former rectory (built in 1936) of St Matthew's opposite the church and changed it into a police station. The house was not really suitable for that use and so it was finally decided to pull it down and build a new station on the same site.

During the next stage the station became a building site, using some containers in which the Gardaí tried their best to do their job during the construction of the new station.

The finished building is state-of-the-art and arguably the most spacious and modern Garda station in a Dublin suburb.

The glass tower at the corner gives a light and airy look to the inside and improves the air circulation. A stained glass window by Elke Westen helps to ease the severe impression of the stark lines. The building includes offices, staff rooms, a small kitchen and some cells both for adults and for adolescents. Cells for adults include beds whereas those for adolescents do not as it is supposed that the parents of the delinquents will have come to collect their erring offspring before nightfall.

Irishtown Garda Station during construction.

The new Irishtown Garda Station.

OTHER BUILDINGS

In the eighteenth and early nineteenth century, Irishtown was known as a seaside village like Ringsend. The beach of Irishtown stretched from Murphy's Baths on its border to Ringsend in the north to Cranfield's Baths at its border to Sandymount in the south. Sea and strand caused quite a few residences to be built. The 1837 map shows some of their names: Pleasant View, Bayview, Tritonville Cottage, Erith Cottage, Erith Lodge and Tritonville Lodge. The 1865 map adds Pembroke Hall and Amanda Ville and on the 1907 map Dodder House and Doddervale Cottage increase the number. Some names are changed, with Amanda Ville for instance mentioned as Cozy Lodge on this map.

One of the oldest buildings in Irishtown is Tritonville Lodge, erected in 1796 and at that stage without any near neighbours. The next building in the direction of Ringsend would have been Irishtown Church, whereas in the Merrion direction it was probably the Conniving House, if that was still there at that stage.

Richard Cranfield (1731–1809), a gilder, wood carver and sculptor, lived in Tritonville Lodge in 1797. The house might have been built for him. He was the founder and owner of Cranfield's Bath. It is not clear how long Tritonville Lodge remained a private residence. There are reports of use for some time by customs officials, as it provided a good view across all of Dublin Bay from Howth to Killiney. On a clear day it would have been easy to see approaching ships from Tritonville Lodge even when they were still far away.

Tritonville Lodge still might have sea views, though definitely not from the ground floor. From the beginning the building has had a wing facing the sea, which is shown on the 1837 OS map, though its shape then seems to have been slightly different from the shape that it has today.

In general Irishtown does not bring grand houses to mind. Seen from the right corner, it looks like a typical Irish village with colourful houses on rather narrow streets, and old village shops.

The letterbox in front of the former shop is some decades younger than the Victorian one in Ringsend, displaying the monogram of George V, who was the last monarch to be called King of Ireland. Letterboxes with that monogram are not very common in this area. Irishtown obviously had not been regarded as important enough to deserve a letterbox under Victoria and Edward VII.

In some of the local lanes the houses are rather old and small, but they are kept in good order. Some of them have raised their roofs to accommodate a

Letterbox in Irishtown with the monogram of George V.

second storey with dormer windows and oblique ceilings. From the address Herbert Place it can be assumed that this lane was developed by or at least named after Sidney Herbert, First Baron of Lea, who died in 1861. Irishtown also has bigger houses, even in its older part.

One of those houses is not only one of the biggest in the centre of Irishtown, it is one of the oldest, shown already in the 1837 OS map on the same spot, even though Pembroke Street was only partly developed by then. Another old house is situated at the border to Ringsend. On the 1837 OS map it looks like a nearly square block of buildings with the name Pleasant View. Since then it has been rebuilt at least once. The more modern building around the corner is now a pub.

The shop at the corner of Irishtown Road and Dodder Terrace was according to Archiseek[15] built with George L. O'Connor as architect in 1915. It is, however, shown on the 1907 OS map already. It might look old-fashioned but is well liked by the locals.

Like every Irish village Irishtown has pubs.

Some of the narrow lanes still seem to look the same way they looked more than 100 years ago. One, going from Irishtown Road past the side of the Beach Tavern to Bath Street, is at least 190 years old, as it is shown on the 1837 map. It might even be older than that.

Following that lane eastwards from the old police station, a familiar advertisement for Guinness from long ago appears to be freshly repainted on the chimney of the pub.

Another public house, a protected structure, is situated on the corner of Barrack Lane with Irishtown Road, just opposite the corner that is occupied by the former police barracks, and it combines a pub with a specialised shop. The same family ran a more general shop further down that lane.

Beach Road, Irishtown.

Barrack Lane,
Irishtown.

Irishtown Road,
at the corner with
Barrack Lane.

Strasburg Terrace.

Village scene in
Irishtown.

Near the border with Ringsend, but still in Irishtown, is a terrace of
villa-styled residences called Strasburg Terrace. This could indicate that
those houses were built around 1871 after the Franco-Prussian War.

Josephine Murray lived here, an aunt of James Joyce. She was the person
whom he asked about the types of trees around the Star of the Sea Church
and the number of steps from the church to the strand. The answer to this
question was not the only topographical detail that she was asked to send
to her nephew.

Despite being a suburb of Dublin and not far from the centre of Ireland's
capital city, Irishtown still has village characteristics, with washing on the
clotheslines visible from the main road, but also has hanging flower baskets
beside the windows.

Mouth of the Swan River.

Former Sewage pumping station.

Two locations in Irishtown must be mentioned, although originally they were most likely not liked very much. One is the mouth of the little Swan River into the Dodder, slightly upriver from Londonbridge. The Swan is a small tributary of the Dodder which like most of those streams in former times was used as a convenient sewer. It was finally culverted, partly to stop it flooding, but also to reduce the stink.

The second spot has to do with sewage as well: the Londonbridge Pumping Station, which was closed in 1985 after 104 years of service. At this pumping station the sewage of Pembroke Township was pumped up into the higher-lying sewage pipes of the Rathmines and Rathgar Township. The combined sewage was then pumped to Poolbeg on the South Wall and released into the sea at receding tides. Nowadays it is at least treated first. The site of this station later was used as a Bring Centre, but that is also now closed.

On the other side of the Dodder was the Morgue, nearly exactly opposite the pumping station on Beggarsbush townland which is regarded as part of Irishtown now.

The current sewage works are on the Poolbeg Peninsula on reclaimed land near the famous landmark of the 'Twin Barber Poles', locally also known as 'The Stacks', the chimneys of the oil-burning power station which in 1971 replaced the old coal-fired power station of 1903. This coal-fired power station was the country's earliest major power production facility and the world's first three-phase generating station. Now, more than 100 years later the power station has been modernised and uses natural gas as fuel. The two chimneys are no longer necessary. The Electricity Supply Board (ESB), their owner, has finally decided to preserve them, as they are a landmark for many Dubliners returning from foreign places by plane or ferry. Since 2014 the chimneys have been protected structures. With a height of 207.5m and 207.8m they are among the tallest man-made structures in Ireland. Apart from some radio transmitting structures, only the Moneypoint Power Station chimneys in County Clare are taller.

Irishtown is an inner suburb of a big city, but there are corners that make you forget this. Some years ago a view from the Railway Bridge down the Dodder, which separates Irishtown from Sandymount, showed a truly rural scene. Flood protection measures along the Dodder later changed this look.

Now after building new walkways along the Dodder walking is easier but nature has moved a bit further away.

Poolbeg chimneys when still in use.

ECONOMY OF IRISHTOWN

The main local 'industry' in Irishtown was fishing, especially the collection of shellfish. Shrimp had been very common on the strand until they disappeared in the severe winter of 1741, which was called 'The hard frost'. Cockles are still abundant and were collected and eaten until the second half of the twentieth century by locals, but pollution put an end to that. Some years ago a noticeboard on Sandymount Strand announced that cockles collected there were not fit for human consumption. During recent years, in which the pollution of Dublin Bay has decreased, a similar board asks anybody collecting cockles on the strand to ring a given telephone number to enquire if it is safe to eat them. The reason for this is the fact that shellfish can accumulate and survive concentrations of pollutants that are lethal for humans, making consumption highly dangerous.

Another activity connected with the sea became commercialised: sea bathing. Irishtown had two baths. At the northern strand of the village, just at the end of what now is Strasburg Terrace, was Murphy's Baths, in John Rocque's map of the City and County of Dublin (1756) described as 'Bath for Women'. (The Bath for Men on that map is shown in Ringsend). Murphy's Baths are shown on the 1837 and 1865 map but on the latter the name is not given. On the 1907 map they have disappeared. Cranfield's Baths were further south, at the north-east corner of what is now Cranfield Place. Those baths were much frequented in the nineteenth century, advertised as: 'Large Swimming Baths for Gentlemen and Separate Swimming Bath for Ladies with Constant and Unlimited Supply of Pure Sea Water Pumped in Directly by Steam Power.'[16] They also had hot or cold reclining baths, hot or cold shower baths and douche baths. Cranfield's Baths are said to have been demolished in 1908 but are not shown on the 1907 map. They were indoor baths, but situated nearly directly at the sea as until the mid-twentieth century Strand Street actually ended on the strand. The area of Irishtown Stadium and the site of the houses north of Seán Moore Road were only reclaimed from the sea in the 1940s.

People who could not afford the entrance fees for the baths still could swim in the sea. Ladies would definitely change in a bathing box. In England these were on wheels and could be pushed into the water, whereas in Irishtown they were fixed on the strand and the bathers had to walk in their swimming costumes across the sand into the water, past whosoever else was on the strand. The price for the use of a bathing box was 1d in Irishtown, whereas in the more affluent villages of Sandymount and Merrion, bathers had to pay 2d to rent one. Earlier, in the eighteenth century, the areas where ladies and gentlemen swam were separated by a good distance as men tended to swim naked.

Until the end of the nineteenth century the buildings of Irishtown village were nearly exclusively situated between the sea in the east, Tritonville Road in the south, Irishtown Road in the west and Strand Road in the north. The 1837 OS map shows hardly any buildings west of Irishtown Road on the stretch between Watery Lane, now Dermot O'Hurley Avenue, and Newbridge Avenue. London Bridge already existed in the early nineteenth century and is described on old maps as 'wooden bridge'. The 1837 map mentions the name 'London Br.' with the further remark 'No Road on Br.' The 1907 map shows houses on Dodder Terrace and Londonbridge Road, both west of Irishtown Road. Most of the land west of Irishtown Road even then was still empty.

Irishtown was mainly a place for people working somewhere else, apart perhaps from a few families occupied with fishing. The first bigger installation that could be regarded as industrial was the Londonbridge Pumping Station of the Rathmines and Pembroke drainage system. It began working in 1881 and lasted until 1985, the first 72 years with the original pumping equipment.[17]

If following the old border between Ringsend and Irishtown eastwards across the reclaimed land, the main part of the Poolbeg Peninsula should be attributed to Irishtown, increasing this village's area and industrial potential enormously. In many cases firms located there give their address as 'Ringsend'. The Irish Glass Bottle Company (started in 1871) employed 1,200 people in its heyday and made millions of bottles before it closed in 2002. This now defunct company might have started in Ringsend, but during its last decades it occupied a big area in Irishtown on grounds that still lie waste, though plans for their development are in place since 2016.

The 1955 Official Industrial Directory or Ireland lists Irish Art Plaster Co., Ltd in Bath Street, Irishtown, under the heading 'religious statues' as well as under 'souvenirs (plaster)'. This company no longer exists. In her book about growing up in Irishtown Angeline Kearns Blain mentions that the firm opened around 1951 in what had been a horse stable. According to her it was owned by an Englishman who employed only people between the age of fourteen and forty. The younger worker then earned 20s for a six-day week.[18]

Today there are some businesses in Irishtown that cannot be found in many other places. The old Dublin Metropolitan Police (DMP) barracks for instance now houses a firm with a studio for producing television and radio commercials. A shop beside Irishtown green provides physiotherapy equipment not only for private patients, but also for physiotherapists and hospitals. There was also a very good picture framing shop called Phoenix Framers in Irishtown, but some years ago it moved to Sandymount.

SPORT FACILITIES

It might astonish many Dubliners to hear that Irishtown has famous sport facilities. This is partly because even Dubliners living in Dublin 4 have only a vague idea about Irishtown and its borders. Obviously a well-known name does not help. Irishtown Stadium is an attraction for many soccer and athletic clubs with its pitches, running tracks and gym. It is owned and run by Dublin City Council now but it was built by Shelbourne FC. Despite the name, many people, when asked, would say that Irishtown Stadium is in

Ringsend. Even Dublin City Council, the owner of the stadium, is not too sure where it is situated. One of its websites says:

> Welcome to Sports & Fitness Irishtown. We are a multi purpose facility in the heart of Ringsend only a few minutes from Dublin City Centre, with plenty of on site parking.[19]

However, on the page of Dublin City's website that lists the fees for the use of Irishtown Stadium or parts of it, the address is given as 'Irishtown Stadium, Irishtown, Dublin 4'.[20] Even if Irishtown is sometimes regarded as part of Ringsend, to insist that Irishtown Stadium is 'in the heart of Ringsend' is misleading to say the least.

The Aviva Stadium situation is similar, considering that according to its website it 'is located in the Ballsbridge suburb of Dublin'.[21] Perhaps this is more understandable as the stadium is situated in the townland of Beggarsbush, which at the time when the first Lansdowne Road Stadium was built was hardly populated at all. The railway line that cuts through the southern corner of the townland was the parish border between the Donnybrook and Irishtown parish of St Mary and the Ballsbridge parish of St Bartholomew, since the time the latter parish was formed. The small part of Beggarsbush west of the railway therefore should be regarded as being part of the parish of St Bartholomew, Ballsbridge, whereas the rest belongs to the parish of St Mary's, Donnybrook, combined with St Matthew's, Irishtown. In this view the Aviva Stadium, which is situated east of the railway, has to be regarded as being situated in Irishtown. There is only one small part, the entrance from Lansdowne Lane, which is west of the railway and therefore could be regarded as situated in Ballsbridge.

Aviva (formerly Lansdowne Road) Stadium, the national rugby and soccer stadium, has developed enormously from Henry Wallace Doveton Dunlop's Royal Park Stadium, which he erected on grounds leased from the Pembroke Estate in December 1872 for sport activities.

Probably the most impressive entrance to this astounding stadium is the Lansdowne Lane entrance, accessed from the Ballsbridge side of the railway.

Whenever there is an event in the Aviva Stadium, either a match or a concert, traffic in the whole area tends to become chaotic. Whole roads are blocked and the Gardaí are out in force.

Aviva Stadium from Irishtown Garda Station.

IRISHTOWN PEOPLE

Some people seem to think that Irishtown is not a good address. In 2013 the Dublin Public Libraries choose *Strumpet City* by James Plunkett as the book in their *One city – one book* month of April. Most sources insist that James Plunkett, whose full name was James Plunkett Kelly, was born in Dublin. Sometimes it is mentioned that he was born in Sandymount. Only very few mention the truth: he was born in 20 Bath Street, Irishtown. When he was born in May 1920, Irishtown was not part of Dublin, but still part of Pembroke Urban District in County Dublin.

Richard Cranfield has been mentioned already. In Irishtown he is known as the founder and proprietor of the baths that were named after him. His artistic career is less well known. In 1756 he was awarded a premium of six pounds by the Royal Dublin Society for a sculpture he had created. In 1765 he sent an *Emblematical Group of Hibernia* carved in wood, executed for the Hibernian Silk Warehouse, to the exhibition of the Society of Artists in George's Lane. At the same exhibition Cranfield also showed a bas-relief in wood of 'Elijah taken up into Heaven'; and the following year he exhibited a 'Group of Boys representing Painting, Sculpture, and Architecture'. He also participated in exhibitions in 1767, 1768, and 1769. He worked as a carver in the Royal Dublin Society's premises in Grafton Street and in 1767 carved 'the new chair for the Society's presiding member'.[22] This chair is still in use in the Ballsbridge premises of the Royal Dublin Society (RDS). In 1771 he was engaged in carving and gilding in the Trinity College Provost's House in Grafton Street, and in the Blue Coat School (now the headquarters of the Law Society).

Another person who was connected to Irishtown was Robert Baker Stoney. He was ordained a priest (Church of Ireland) in 1864 and officiated in this area from 1864 when he became curate of Taney Parish in Dundrum. In his subsequent positions he was a curate in the parish of St Mary's in Donnybrook from 1868 to 1872, and in 1872, when the parish of St Matthew's, Irishtown, was established, he became the first incumbent of this new parish. In 1887 he was nominated Acting Chaplain to the Troops at the Pigeon House Fort. In 1893 he was appointed Canon of Christ Church Cathedral and in the same year became Chaplain to the Lord Lieutenant in Ireland.[23]

Angela Kearns Blain (b.1938) grew up in Irishtown in poverty and describes in her autobiography[24] the life of a working class family in the 1940s and 1950s, first in Ballsbridge and later in Irishtown. She emigrated to the United States, married and became Adjunct Professor of Sociology and Women's Studies in Boise State University, Idaho.

4

SANDYMOUNT

HISTORICAL REMARKS

Sandymount is different from the other three coastal villages in Dublin 4. At a time when Merrion had grown to become a village and Ringsend to a port and fishing town, Sandymount was an area that was not inhabited – except by birds and foxes, as well as rabbits that had been brought in by the Normans who loved their meat and their fur. They had to build warrens for them because of the foxes. When the warrens decayed and the area became inhabited by humans the rabbits disappeared, but the foxes are still there.

The place was not called Sandymount in former times either. An early name was 'Scald Hill' or 'Scallet Hill', but it is not quite clear what area exactly was called by this name. The name might have something to do with the Irish word 'sceallа' meaning 'shale'[1], which occasionally does occur in the surroundings. Scallet Hill must have been an area that was slightly raised. Its highest spot is supposed to be where the Sandymount church of Our Lady, Star of the Sea, was built later. In general the land was a marshy heath with lots of sand, some clay and some shale. There were many little ponds dotted around it as well. This bit of land was probably uninhabited until the beginning of the eighteenth century. Until then it was only used for the rabbit warrens of the Normans and their descendants who in this area from the fifteenth century on were the Fitzwilliams. This family was ennobled in 1629 by the Crown and became Viscounts Fitzwilliam of Merrion and Barons Fitzwilliam of Thorncastle in the Irish nobility.

In those times rabbits were hunted with ferrets driving the rabbits into nets. It is only since the eighteenth century, when the fences around the warrens had decayed, that rabbits became feral in this area. Their number decreased quickly and the number of foxes on the other hand increased.

EARLIEST INDUSTRIES

The coast of this area was well known for centuries for its herring fishery. Some of the partly swampy, partly sandy land adjacent to the sea also became of use at the beginning of the eighteenth century because its clay was of a quality suitable to make bricks. The landlords of the area, the Viscounts Fitzwilliam, consequently started a brick industry in 1731 as loads of bricks were necessary for the development of that part of their estate which now is within the Dublin 2 area, where houses were built on Merrion Square and Fitzwilliam Square as well as on the streets around them. In those times the area from Scallet Hill southwards to Merrion and including the seaside half of Merrion townland became known as Lord Merrion's Brickfields. One of the clay pits was in the area of today's Sandymount Green and the workers lived in cottages around a common near their work.

People moved into this area and started a settlement that became known as Brickfields or Brickfield Town. This brick industry lowered the already low-lying ground of the area by up to 2m, so that many parts of Sandymount are now below high water mark. To protect his property Richard, Seventh Viscount Fitzwilliam, built a wall from Merrion Gates to Prospect Terrace in 1791. The wall is still there, the longest and one of the oldest man-made structures in the area.

Brickmaking was a seasonal occupation; the brickfields were worked from April to September. The first step was to dig the clay and leave it for a few days. It was then tempered by moistening and trampling. After that the bricks were put into moulds to harden and were finally fired.[2]

As long as the brick industry was going, which was for around sixty years, it gave employment to a number of families. According to a return for the parish of St Mary, Donnybrook, ten families lived in 'Brickfields' in 1766, half of them Protestant, the other half 'Papist'. Such a number of inhabitants makes the word 'town' in Brickfield Town a bit too grandiose. At the same time there were 103 families each in Ringsend (with a Protestant majority) and Irishtown (with a Catholic majority).[3] When the clay deposit was exhausted, the pits were filled in and the common eventually turned into Sandymount Green.

Another industry was probably not as generally respected as Lord Fitzwilliam's brickfields though it would bring in more revenue. In the north-western corner of Sandymount, south of where Herbert Bridge is now, Haig's Distillery was situated. It was also known as Dodderbank Distillery. At that time there was no bridge yet at this place and people wanting to cross the river had to use a weir right beside the distillery. According to the

Pembroke Papers, held by the National Archives, Robert Haig leased land with a date of 2 August 1813 for 99 years from 'the Rt. Hon. Richard Lord Viscount Fitzwilliam of Merryon' for £234.12.0 p.a.[4] There must have been an earlier lease, as Haig bought the distillery in 1795.

Kevin P. O'Rourke mentions in his talk 'From Scallet Hill to Brickfield Town' read to the Old Dublin Society in 1985 that there was no connection of the owner John Haig of that distillery with the Scottish distillers of the same name, while other authors are convinced that the owners of the two distilleries were cousins of some sort. The old cemetery of Donnybrook (in Donnybrook Road)provides some information. The owner of the Sandymount distillery is buried there and the headstone makes it quite clear that not only was there a Scottish connection but that the first name of this distiller was not John, but Robert. There actually was a John Haig in the family, one of the sons of Robert Haig, but this John died in 1837, aged 36, eight years before his father. The family were descendants of the Lairds of Bemersyde in Berwickshire. The inscription on this headstone reads:

SACRED TO THE MEMORY OF
ROBERT HAIG OF ROEBUCK
AND DODDERBANK IN THE COUNTY OF DUBLIN DISTILLER
(SIXTH IN DESCENT FROM
JAMES HAIG OF BEMERSYDE BERWICKSHIRE)
BORN IN CLACKMANNANSHIRE 4TH APRIL 1764
DIED 19TH AUGUST 1845 AGED 81 YEARS AND WAS BURIED HERE

ALSO OF CAROLYNE MARY HIS WIFE, DAUGHTER OF
SIR WM WOLSELEY BARONET OF WOLSELEY STAFFORDHIRE

DIED AT ROEBUCK 10TH JULY 1833 AGED 54 YEARS
AND WAS BURIED HERE.

THEY HAD ISSUE THIRTEEN CHILDREN THREE OF WHOM
DIED IN INFANCY
SEVEN SONS AND THREE DAUGHTERS SURVIVED
AND ALL MARRIED

The website 'The Haig Family Story'[5] gives information about the children of an older John Haig and Margaret Stein (the Steins were another Scottish distilling family). This list mentions a daughter Margaret, who married John Jameson, later of Dublin, and a son Robert who 'moved to Dublin where he purchased Dodderbank Distillery in 1795'. The dates of birth and death as well as the year in which Robert Haig started distilling in Dublin fit in with data about him in local records. This website also shows that Robert was an uncle of the John Haig who founded the John Haig & Co. Ltd Distillery in Scotland and that Robert Haig was the brother-in-law of John Jameson.

According to the gravestone Robert Haig had a big family. John Russell[6] mentions the Dublin branch of the huge Haig family including the fact that Robert Haig's children had issues, some of whom married other Haigs.

Around 1800 Robert Haig's Dodderbank Distillery was the second biggest distillery in Dublin. After that the brothers John, William and James Jameson arrived in Dublin from Scotland (a fourth brother, Alexander, started a distillery in Enniscorthy, Co. Wexford) and founded distilleries that like those of the Power and Roe families became important firms. By 1822 Robert Haig's business was the fifth biggest distillery in Dublin according to output, behind the three distilleries of the Jameson brothers and that of John Power.

In the following years the distilling industry declined. The economic situation in Ireland in the mid-nineteenth century was suffering badly from the famine and distilling also from the temperance movement. Changes in tax and excise laws did not help. Robert Haig died in 1845. He had been in a constant battle with revenue as long as he worked the distillery and he finally lost. The men formerly employed by him lost their income. Even Mother Mary Aikenhead (founder of the Religious Sisters of Charity), who was no advocate of strong drink, bemoaned the loss of jobs, though she mentioned that the distillery employed eight families, which is a surprisingly low number for such a labour-intensive industry. She reported this loss of employment in 1833, but it is not clear if the distillery closed in that year or if they just had to reduce staff for some time, as other sources report that in that year Robert Haig introduced a Coffey still into his distillery. This might be a printer's error as far as the year is concerned, as it is known that the Dodderbank Distillery vastly increased its output in 1823. It is likely that it actually was this year and not 1833 in which the Coffey still was installed. The distillery is still shown on the OS map of 1837, but was taken down in the following years and some of its material was used for the foundation of buildings in the development of Herbert Road and Newbridge Avenue. The 'new bridge' was Herbert Bridge, built at the spot where a weir in the Dodder had been before, which up to the building of the bridge had been used to cross the river from Lansdowne Road (formerly Haig's Lane) to reach what is now Newbridge Avenue.

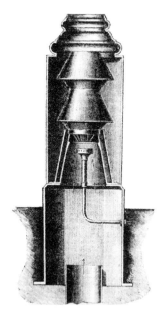

Holman's Sewer Gas Destructor
in Park Avenue, near St John's
church.

Not an industry, but a very early industrial product to improve air quality
can be found in Park Avenue: a Holman's (sometimes called Keeling's) sewer
gas destructor. Those destructors could be built into the foot of a lamppost,
as it has been done here.

The working of these destructors is described in *The British Medical
Journal*, 17 March 1888, p. 618, which also describes tests concerning their
efficiency and economy.[7]

DEVELOPMENT OF BIG HOUSES

When it could be foreseen that brickmaking soon would stop because of
lack of the raw material, clay, Lord Fitzwilliam planned to develop his lands
as residential area. Sea-bathing had become fashionable; the viscount took
advantage of that and started to advertise his grounds near the sea. He
gathered that the people in his target group would not come to live in a place
called 'Bricktown' or similar, so he changed the name of the settlement and
from the end of the eighteenth century it was called Sandymount. Richard
Lewis's entry shows that this plan worked.

SANDY MOUNT. A very pleasant little village, three quarters of a mile
to the right of Ringsend, and two miles from the Castle of Dublin. There
are many elegant villas and sweet retreats at this place, chiefly belonging
to the Citizens of Dublin.[8]

R. Lewis published his guide in 1787, at a time when the brick industry was
in decline. None of the houses that he had noticed seem to have survived.
Roslyn Park, built in 1789, now is regarded as the oldest building in
Sandymount. Around thirty years after Lewis another author connects the
growth of Sandymount with sea-bathing:

SANDYMOUNT, which is large and populous compared with Irishtown,
has of late years been the principle resort of the city-bathers.[9]

Residences mentioned on OS maps of 1837 are from north to south
Mountain View, Seafield, Laburnum Lodge, Elm Villa, Diana Cottage,
Serpentine Lodge, Sandymount House, Beech Grove, Belvidere House,
Willfield, Lakelands, Park View and Flood Villa.

Some big houses built at that time still exist. Sandymount Park, not
named on the map, was one of those. It was built in 1788–89 and changed
names and owners a couple of times. It now is a part of the Rehab complex
and is called Roslyn Park. It was built for the artist William Ashford, an
Englishman who came to Ireland aged 18. After he had established himself
in Dublin he lived in a house on College Green:

Ashford afterwards sold his house in College-green, and retired to
Sandymount, a residence more suitable to his habits and taste of a
landscape-painter. His noble friend, Viscount Fitzwilliam, the lord of the
soil, not only gave him a lease of ground on very moderate terms, but
strongly urged him to erect a villa upon it for himself, which he did in a
very appropriate style, and with considerable taste, for which his friend Mr
Gandon gave him a suitable design. In this residence, Sandymount-park, he
pursued his profession with indefatigable industry, painting, both in oil and
water-colour, the 'counterfeit presentment' of much of the finest scenery of
England, Wales, and Ireland. He was one of the three artists to whom their
brethren paid the distinguished compliment of confiding the selection of
eleven others with themselves to constitute the Royal Hibernian Academy,
when incorporated by charter of George IV.[10]

Gandon Villa.

The 1907 OS map shows two houses on this site, one of which is described as Rosslyn Park, the other as Sandymount Park. At some time both buildings were referred to as Sandymount Park, the Gandon villa taking this name first, being renamed later as Sandymount Park House, then Park House and then Rosslyn Park. Its entrance and gate lodge were on Beach Road. The other building in the same park was also called Sandymount Park and contrary to the Gandon villa kept that name. Its address was 28 Newgrove Avenue as its entrance was from this road. The Gandon-designed house was for some time the home of the fish and poultry merchant family Dunn. Dick Humphreys, famous for winning many motorcycle races (e.g. the Isle of Man T.T.) lived there in the years 1929–33.[11] From 1950 to 1982 it housed a secondary school for girls run by the Sisters of the Sacred Heart of Mary. After that it housed the headquarters of the Rehab charity who sold it in 2016 to the Department of Education, which will use it to build primary and secondary schools. Locally Roslyn Park is known as 'The House with the Eggcup on Top'.

Sandymount green is the centre of Sandymount with Sandymount 'Castle' on one side and a number of shops on the other two sides. Sandymount Castle would be of similar age as Roslyn Park. It is mentioned in S. Lewis[12] as the residence of R. Corbett, a great-uncle of William Butler Yeats on his mother's side. Both W.B. Yeats's father (the artist John Yeats) and grandfather lived there for some time. The railings around the Green were erected in Corbett's time. The huge horse chestnut trees, however, were planted at the beginning of the twentieth century, contrary to the belief of some local historians who think that these trees also go back to Corbett's initiative.

Corbett had put substantial money into the house and the park, but later – perhaps because of that – he got into financial difficulties and became bankrupt. In 1870 he committed suicide by jumping from the mail-boat that ran between Holyhead and Dun Laoghaire.[13]

Sandymount Castle's street front on Sandymount Green is less interesting than the garden frontage. The OS maps of 1837 as well as 1865 show the house to have a long garden with an ornamental pond on the south side of the castle (away from the Green) reaching down to Lakelands (on what now is Gilford Road). This garden is still shown on the OS map of 1907, but in that year the water feature had disappeared. The whole garden was developed in the second half of the twentieth century and houses on that ground now have the addresses Sandymount Castle Park, Sandymount Castle Road and Sandymount Castle Drive. According to the 1901 and 1911 censuses Sandymount Castle was used as a school in the first years of the twentieth century.

Today the building known as Sandymount Castle is divided into different dwellings, which are easily told apart by the different colours of their facades.

Sandymount Castle from Sandymount Green.

The houses next to Sandymount Castle, called Castleville and Castleton, are similar in look to Sandymount Castle, but smaller in size. The colour contrast between houses on this side of Sandymount Green can be striking.

Another residence mentioned by Lewis is Wilfield House in Sandymount Avenue. Like Sandymount Castle it is probably from around 1800, although there is a possibility that it includes earlier parts.

Castleville.

Wilfield House.

Direct neighbours of Wilfield House are other old houses. S. Lewis[14] mentions N. Anderson, Esq. as living in Wilfield House in 1837, whereas Nathaniel Anderson, tobacco merchant, and most likely the same person is reported as owner of Wilfield Cottage in *The Roads to Sandymount, Irishtown, Ringsend* in 1834, with Mary, the widow of John Clarke living in it. John Clarke had died in this house in 1831. At the beginning of the 1880s a list of subscribers for the Dean O'Connell Memorial in the Roman Catholic Church of Our Lady, Star of the Sea, mentions John C. Murphy, Esq., of Wilfield House who donated £4, and Miss Murphy, who donated £3,[15] sizeable sums of money at that time. There also were more buildings on the site called Willfield, stretching out from Wilfield House towards the railway. Besides Wilfield House, Wilfield Gate Lodge (Mrs Lane) and Wilfield Cottage (Miss Lane) are mentioned in 1884.

Both the 1837 and the 1907 OS maps show two different big buildings. The 1837 map calls the whole complex Willfield; the 1907 map however calls the bigger building to the south-west Willfield and the dwelling towards the north-east Willfield House. The latter name is not mentioned in 1837, but the footprint of the building is like the one on the 1907 map and the way it still is today.

The dwelling south-west of Wilfield House is quite a big complex, now called Gilford House. On the old maps some other, smaller structures are shown around those two bigger buildings. There still is a Wilfield Lodge, but it looks like a modern building set back between Wilfield House and Gilford House.

A big park-like garden stretched towards the south-west in the direction of the railway, but not quite reaching it. When in 1933 the lease for this garden of Wilfield (Gilford House) ran out, a builder leased the area from the Pembroke Estate and developed it into a complete new road named Wilfield Park.

Belvidere House is one of the few buildings on Sandymount Strand shown on the 1837 OS map. The 1907 map shows it as a big building, divided into two plots. Today there is still a big house on that site with its front to the sea, but this is much-extended compared with the building shown on the 1907 map. It is in apartments now and a more modern block of apartments has been built on the north-western corner of it.

The 1837 map shows a big garden north and south of Belvidere House. When house-numbering started Belvidere House became No. 43. Numbers 41 and 45 were quite a distance away then, indicating that there was still a lot of ground belonging to No. 43. Nowadays all that is gone and the quite sizeable houses south of No. 43 have the numbers 43 b, c, d, e, f and g.

43 Strand Road (formerly Belvidere House).

The age of Claremont House is unknown. It is not mentioned in S. Lewis. Some sources say it was built in the 1790s,[16] although the 1837 OS map shows no building where Claremont House is now. It is, however, shown on the OS map of 1875. The OS map of 1907 shows the house standing on its own, without direct neighbours. It was reached by a slightly curved drive from a lodge on Claremont Road, as well as from another lodge on Sandymount Road.

The house is still in the same place, with the same footprint as in 1875 and the drive from Claremont Road is also still there, but this has been considerably widened and many houses were built on either side of the drive and beside the house itself during the last sixty years. There is no access from Sandymount Road to Claremont House anymore.

Another 'castle' in Sandymount is even younger. Holyrood Castle as it stands now was built in the 1880s and today is divided into four luxury apartments. An earlier Castle Kennedy is shown on Ordinance Survey maps of the area in 1868 and 1870 on the same spot. It is mentioned as it is on the Sandymount side of the railway, though Holyrood Castle is on Smotscourt townland, as is the Sandymount DART Station. This townland would at least formerly have been attributed to Ballsbridge.

Claremont House.

In the second half of the nineteenth century a special use was considered for Castle Kennedy.

> In 1872, Dublin Corporation proposed that a smallpox hospital be built at Castlekennedy, Sandymount, but the project was fiercely opposed and was eventually dropped and a floating hospital was established in the Pigeon House Harbour.[17]

On the 1837 OS map the whole area south of Sandymount Green and west of Sandymount Tower contained orchards, gardens and fields, with only Lakelands and a couple of more houses (on Park Avenue) interrupting the open ground.

CHURCHES AND RELIGIOUS BUILDINGS

The northernmost church, just at the beginning of Sandymount Road, approached from Newbridge Avenue, is the Roman Catholic Parish Church of Our Lady, Star of the Sea, locally known as 'The Star'. Its foundation stone was laid on 7 May 1851, on a site between Sandymount and Irishtown, actually just across the townland border, which means that officially it is situated in Irishtown, as the old chapel it replaced.[18] At the time when it was built it seems to have been important that the new chapel should be in the same townland as the old one. Revd N. Donnelly especially mentions that the new chapel was built '… some distance south of the old chapel, but within the same townland of Irishtown …'.[19]

The architect of this church was James Joseph McCarthy, a well-known architect of that time who not only built the Catholic cathedrals of Armagh, Ennis, Killarney and Monaghan, but in Dublin also St Saviour's in Dominic Street and St Mary's in Haddington Road. The first stone for the new church was laid on 7 May 1851, by the Most Revd Daniel Murray, Archbishop of Dublin. A year-and-a-half later disaster struck:

> In Christmas week of 1852 a terrific storm raged for two or three days over and around Dublin. Trees, roofs, and entire houses were demolished by it, and many accidents to life and limb were reported. The new church did not escape. It was ready for roofing when the storm burst, and front and rear gables, with their elaborate Gothic windows, went down before it. Renewed efforts were promptly made to repair the disaster, the cost of which, however, had to fall to the most part on the contractor.[20]

The Church of Our Lady, Star of the Sea ('The Star'), Sandymount.

Star of the Sea from Sandymount Road, 1884.

During the first decades of its existence The Star was a chapel of ease for St Mary's, Haddington Road, the parish church of the Roman Catholic Parish of Irishtown and Donnybrook. It became a parish church in 1876, when Sandymount was split from Haddington Road.

Nowadays the church is surrounded by trees and houses, making it difficult to photograph. Originally it was much easier to see, as there were no trees around it and the sea was much nearer, with the national school not yet built.[21]

The side entrances that were new at that time are not entrances anymore, but have been turned into the parish bookshop on the north side and a chapel on the south side. The vestry and attached bell tower which today are half-hidden by trees originally had been planned as a base to a much bigger tower with a steeple. Another view shows the steps down to Sandymount Strand as James Joyce remembered and described them in his *Ulysses*.

Originally this church was rather dark inside. Today the inside of 'The Star' is bright and cheerful, with a clear view up into the timber beams of the roof. In that it looks similar to St Patrick's in Ringsend, but Sandymount sticks to tradition in the sense that the altar is at the east end.

Contrary to churches of the medieval Gothic, the big west window in this Neo-Gothic church does not have stained glass, but then the inside view of it is blocked by the organ.

Joshua Clarke's studio provided some of the stained glass windows, one of which shows the signature of Joshua. Ken Ryan, managing director of

Star of the Sea from Sandymount Strand 1884.

Abbey Stained Glass Studios kindly supplied information about the costs of the windows by Joshua Clarke:

Order Book 1 Page 62 18 December 1912
Very Revd C Ridgeway, PP Sandymount.
Chancel gable and side chapel windows as per estimate 17 December 1912
1 chancel, 1 gable @ £3.17.6 each £7.15.0
2 side chapels @ £3.7.6 each £6.15.0

The sum of £ 14 10s 0d translates into decimal coinage as £14.50. Today's equivalent of this is around €2,000. Considering that in 1880 Pembroke Township had paid the sum of £75 (equivalent to €11,000) for the stained glass window of two lights in the staircase of the Town Hall, Joshua Clarke's prices seem to have been quite low.

Originally Sandymount had a Presbyterian church, which stood directly opposite the Star of the Sea. As the townland border at that stretch runs in the middle of Sandymount Road, this church actually stood on Sandymount townland.

This Presbyterian church was built by three brothers Hay as architects (from Liverpool) and completed in 1858, only a few years later than the Star. It stood empty since 1975 when the Presbyterian congregation agreed with the Methodist congregation that they would share the little church at Sandymount Green. Despite many protests it was demolished in 1999 and replaced by living accommodation.

One of the three corners of Sandymount Green is occupied by a church that is indisputably situated in Sandymount: Christ Church, the Methodist church which, after the demolition of the former Presbyterian church opposite the Star of the Sea in 1999, is jointly used by Methodists and Presbyterians.Its architect was Alfred Gresham Jones who later built Mytilene (No. 53 Ailesbury Road in Donnybrook, now residence of the French ambassador). The church was opened in 1864, transepts were added in 1872, an organ in 1908 and the little porch in 1911.[22]

With the Roman Catholic church on the northern end towards Irishtown, Sandymount also has a church on the opposite southern end, towards Merrion: St John the Evangelist. This Anglican church was built on the instruction of Sidney Herbert, who also carried all the costs. The architect was Benjamin Ferrey. The website of the church[23] says that it is 'unusual if not unique' as it does not have a parish.

The church originally was ornamented with many monsters and gargoyles, especially on its roof, but the then archbishop of Dublin objected to these and they had to be removed. The grinning beasties of the chimney escaped His Grace's displeasure, perhaps because the chimney was on the vestry and not the church proper.

St John the Evangelist, Sandymount.

Inside there are not only good stained glass windows, some of the oldest in the area, others by Joshua Clarke, but also a beautiful mosaic on the eastern wall. This is from the beginning of the twentieth century and described as: '... the magnificent Armstrong memorial mosaic which is a strikingly successful twentieth-century enhancement of Ferrey's original design.'[24]

The same source mentions the altar frontal and banners that were produced by the first Anglican order of sisters in Ireland, known as the Community of St John the Evangelist, who had their community house nearby. It was later sold and has by now been replaced by a residential complex.

Both the Fitzwilliams and the Pembrokes were absentee landlords and used agents to look after their Irish estates. In the second half of the eighteenth century Bryan Fagan was the agent for the Viscounts Fitzwilliam and after him his wife Elizabeth, followed by their daughter Barbara, who married Richard Verschoyle. This couple were trusted so much that according to the will of Richard, Seventh Viscount Fitzwilliam, they had the use of Mount Merrion House for themselves and their descendants.[25] The Herbert family, Earls of Pembroke and heirs of the Viscounts Fitzwilliam kept the Verschoyles on as agents. They lived in Mount Merrion House which was in the (Anglican) parish of Taney, where Richard Verschoyle was a churchwarden in the years

Mosaic in St John the Evangelist, Sandymount.

Altar cloth, St John the Evangelist, Sandymount.

1798–99 and 1811–13. Barbara Verschoyle née Fagan continued as agent of the Pembroke Estate after her parents were gone, first with her husband Richard and after his death in 1827 on her own, despite the fact that she was not only a woman, but also a Roman Catholic. For a woman to fill such a post was practically unheard of at that time, so the fact that Barbara Verschoyle worked as agent after her mother Elizabeth Fagan died showed the ability of these ladies, who had earned the trust of their employers, both the Fitzwilliams and the Herberts. Barbara Verschoyle did not only fill the post satisfactory, she also had quite some influence with Sidney Herbert who had inherited the estate. In her trusted position she was able to organise a school for the poor in Sandymount. She asked the Sisters of Charity to help with this school (the exact location of which is lost, but it was on Sandymount Avenue in the area where the health clinic is now, but possibly on the other side of the road) and organised the move of the sisters into the house provided for them in the Sandymount part of what is now Sandymount Avenue.[26]

Not only did Barbara Verschoyle provide a residence for the convent, she donated a chalice to the sisters with the inscription 'Donum Barbarae Verschoyle Conventus Sororum Charitatis Sandymount Fundatricis A.D. 1831. Orate pro ea.' (A gift of Barbara Verschoyle, the foundress of the convent of the Sisters of Charity Sandymount AD 1831. Pray for her) This chalice is no longer in Sandymount. According to Sr Marie Bernadette, General Archives, RSC Caritas, Sandymount, it was passed on to a mission in Africa.

Mother Mary Aikenhead, the foundress of the Religious Sisters of Charity, and four sisters moved into the house on Sandymount Avenue (then still referred to as Sandymount Lane) in 1831 and called the congregation the Convent of the Nativity of Our Blessed Lady. The house had a little chapel that was open to the public but the whole complex was so small that the sisters themselves had to follow Mass in their convent from their parlour.[27]

From this small convent Mother Mary Aikenhead organised relief for the poor during the cholera epidemic in 1832–33 as well as organising the founding of St Vincent's Hospital in St Stephen's Green (which later moved to Elm Park, Merrion) even though at that time she was very sick and did most of the work from her sickbed. She moved into St Vincent's Hospital in St Stephen's Green herself in 1834. In 1845 Mother Aikenhead moved to Harold's Cross which at that time still was in the country. She died in Harold's Cross on Christmas Day 1854 and is buried in the convent graveyard in Donnybrook.[28]

In 1856 Carmelite Nuns from North William Street bought the residence Lakelands which had been a private residence until then. They brought a

Former convent of the Sisters of Charity in Sandymount Lane. (By kind permission of the Sisters of Charity)

school and an orphanage with them which they had run in North William Street. Two years later this institution of the Carmelite Sisters turned into Ireland's first Certified Industrial School, certified for seventy girls. The sisters found running the school not compatible with their way of life in a contemplative order and in 1876 they finally were allowed to swap places with the Sisters of Charity who merged their own little school with the Lakelands school and took over the care of the orphans. The Carmelite Sisters stayed only for a short period in Sandymount Avenue and moved to Roebuck in 1877. They leased the house to the Brothers of St John of God who ran a home for convalescent gentlemen there from 1878 to 1882 when they sub-leased the house to Joseph Boyle who ran a college for young gentlemen in it until the lease ran out in 1887. During the last years of its existence the house seems to have been a private residence. Around 1900 the building was demolished and four redbrick houses were built there which are shown on the 1907 OS map.

The school in Lakelands added new buildings in 1974. The Sisters of Charity ran the school, now called Scoil Mhuire, until 1998 when it was handed over to the parish. Apart from the school the complex has living quarters for the sisters as well as Bethany House, which provides sheltered housing for elderly people.

Franciscan Missionary Sisters for Africa, Generalate, Gilford Road.

Gilford Hall, 13 Gilford Road.

The Franciscan Missionary Sisters for Africa were founded by Mother Kevin (birth name: Teresa Kearney) who was born in Arklow, Co. Wicklow. As the name says, they operate in Africa – working there since 1903, even though Mother Kevin only founded the order in 1952. Their generalate is in Gilford Road in Sandymount, nearly opposite the Sisters of Charity in Lakelands. On the OS map of 1837 this house is not shown yet. On the OS map of 1907 it is shown with the name Dunroe.

Not very far from Dunroe and Lakelands another building in Sandymount was meant as a place for religious meetings: Gilford Hall. In the 1911 census it is described as 'Meeting House and Private Dwelling'. Nowadays it is used commercially and one of the firms that has its office in it mentions on its website that it was built as a Meeting House for the Society of Friends. According to the date on the front gable it was built in 1876.

Sandymount also houses the only Gurdwara of the Sikhs in the Republic of Ireland – the Gurdwara Guru Nanak Darbar on Serpentine Avenue. The building was erected as a cinema and opened in 1936 under the name Astoria, renamed Ritz in 1947 and Oscar in the early 1970s. After film screenings ended in 1976, it became the Oscar Theatre, featuring live performances. In 1985 it closed as a theatre, was sold and subsequently completely restructured inside. As the outside has not been changed it still looks like a cinema.

Gurdwara Guru Nanak Darbar, Serpentine Avenue, Sandymount.

The religion of the Sikhs originated in India. The importance of the Gurdwara for the Sikh community is described as follows:

> The main function of the gurdwara is to provide Sikhs with a meeting-place for worship, consisting of listening/singing to the words of the Guru Granth Sahib, and hearing them expounded in katha, or lectures: The gurdwara also serves as a community centre, a school, a guest house for pilgrims and travellers, and a base for local charitable activities. Dublin Gurdwara is known as Gurdwara Guru Nanak Darbar. It has two main halls, Divan Hall and Langar Hall. Divan Hall is main hall where the holy Guru Granth Sahib is present.[29]

FURTHER GROWTH OF THE VILLAGE

Sandymount green in the centre of Sandymount is a small, (nearly) triangular park on the site of one of the earlier clay pits. Its shape has not changed since the early nineteenth century, as the OS map of 1837 shows. At that time there still were a few gaps between the buildings on its west side, but the other two sides were completely built up already. Sandymount Castle probably dates

Sandymount Green and Sandymount Village.

from around 1800 and Robert Corbett to some extend re-built it during the 1830s in the neo-Gothic style that was in vogue then. The neighbouring buildings on the south side of Sandymount Green were most likely changed or re-built at that time.

In summer the Green is very well favoured by families with young children and, as long as the weather allows, it is used as a place for a restful lunch hour by workers from the shops and offices in the vicinity. It is also used for local gatherings and parties.

The Earl of Pembroke as landlord of Sandymount Green offered it in 1900 as a gift to Pembroke Urban District Council. In 1904 Pembroke UDC added a water fountain between the central bed and the northern corner. Old photographs show that this fountain was more elaborate than the one built in Herbert Park a couple of years later which is still there. Since the 1960s Sandymount Green has been administered by the Parks Department of Dublin City Council. The iron railings around the Green are mentioned by S. Lewis in 1837 and they look as if they still are the original railings of that time.

The fountain that was installed in 1904 has disappeared. In its place is an access chamber with a cast iron cover. The Green still has one of the formerly quite common water pumps in one of its corners. It no longer functions, the handle is missing and it seems to have been equipped with a more modern

Over 50s garden party on Sandymount Green, 22 July 2015.

tap in its later life, considering that the little hole over the original spout is still there, even though the tap itself has disappeared. Today it is thought to be a replacement for an earlier pump.

Everybody knows the protected shopfront of The Lady Chemist, the shop that is still usually referred to as 'Miss Milligan's' by Sandymount locals, even though Miss Milligan is long gone. The shop started as a grocer's, before it became a hardware shop. The hardware shop was run by the eponymous Miss Milligan, who lived nearby at 21 Sandymount Green.

Afterwards it became in turn a bookshop, an estate agent and is now a chemist's shop known as the Lady Chemist to distinguish it from the other chemist in Sandymount. Like many facades in Dublin it changes colour from time to time; over the years it has appeared in different shades of red as well as in black and in a pale olive-green. With all the changes of owners and wares on offer it is understandable that not everybody knows that the original shop was called Fleming's, despite the fact that the name still can be seen in the mosaic floor at the entrance.

The Fleming family ran a grocer's shop and public house in the building that now is known as Sandymount House officially and Ryan's pub locally.

Sandymount Green
with Christmas tree,
Sunday, 11 December
2016.

Water pump on
Sandymount Green.

It is just a pub now and no longer a shop. It has two entrances, one on Sandymount Green and another on Seafort Avenue. These have been there quite a long time and are the reason why in the 1911 census it appears with a different address than in the 1901 census. Another entrance might have been on the corner, but if so, this was closed many years ago.

Around 1900 there were five pubs in Sandymount, now there are three and all of them also serve food. The most obvious one is Sandymount House, as it occupies a corner site. On the 1837 OS map, this building is labelled as 'Sandymount Castle'.

The corner premises of Sandymount Road and Claremont Road was a shop for many decades – first Leverett & Frye, then Bracken's and now Spar. On the first floor of this building there is an Indian restaurant, offering a good view over Seafort Avenue, one of the oldest streets in Sandymount. Seafort Avenue was already completely built up in 1837, including a mansion with a big garden around it and other residences, one of them with the name Laburnum Lodge. The house with the surrounding garden was later taken down and the little houses of Seafort Villas were built on its ground.

The pub now known as Sandymount House at 1 Sandymount Green, is left of Miss Milligan's which now has the address No. 1a, Sandymount Green. Right of this well-known shop we find 2 Sandymount Green, now an Italian restaurant in the building that used to be Findlater's Sandymount shop. That branch of Findlater's opened in 1897 and closed in 1969.

The centre of Sandymount.

The building that used to be Findlater's shop.

Sandymount village and its green have always been well visited. Nowadays with all its offices, shops and pubs, Sandymount is quite vibrant. Around lunchtime and after five o'clock in the afternoon, parking can be a problem for shoppers and people relaxing after work. Some decades ago parking would not have been difficult, as there were few cars around. Shopping then was different. Fifty years ago anybody who had a telephone would do quite an amount of shopping by phone. One had an account with the butcher, the baker, the greengrocer and the dairy shop, the goods were delivered and the bill was paid at the end of the month. In Sandymount some people still have an account with the butcher.

Occasionally a shop may not do so well and one shop in Seafort Avenue has been closed for decades. For years it was an antiques and curio shop with the name 'SPQR'. This old, small shop is part of the area owned by the Rehab Charity. It has stood empty for years and looks more and more dilapidated.

During the last fifteen years the number of restaurants in Sandymount has increased. During the first years of this century there was only a daytime delicatessen with a couple of tables, doing a good takeaway business. This

The former shop in Seafort Avenue in 2004.

The Orchards, formerly Cottage Park House.

has morphed into a proper bistro, but it is no longer the only eating place. All three pubs serve food, one of them in a proper restaurant behind the pub, and apart from that three Italian and an Indian restaurant have appeared, all on or very near Sandymount Green. In 2016 a further restaurant opened with a menu of Irish dishes and dishes showing an Asian influence, but this for some reason did not survive very long. Hopefully a new restaurant will occupy those premises soon.

Like other areas of Dublin 4, Sandymount has what is regarded as 'good addresses'. Railway Union Sports Club, for instance, says that they are in 'the best address in Sandymount: Park Avenue'. Park Avenue originally was called Cottage Park Avenue, after Cottage Park House to which it led. The house is still there, though it is called The Orchards now.

Today there are buildings that might have 'cottage' or 'lodge' in their name, whereas in the estate agents' books they are called 'villas' like in many other well-to-do areas in the Dublin suburbs. Some of those in Park Avenue with names like Park Lodge, Rosevale or Linden Lodge have quite big front gardens, whereas in some other streets more rural-style houses front the road, with perhaps a garden or outhouses in the back behind the house.

One of those so-called villas, now squeezed in between much more modern buildings, is Wilton Lodge in Claremont Road, not far from Sandymount Green. The 1837 map shows a building with the name Serpentine Lodge on

Linden Lodge, Park Avenue.

Gilford Avenue.

this spot. In 1875 as well as in 1907 the OS maps show the house as it is now, with its distinctive steps to the front door.

An entrance in the records of St Matthew's Church, Irishtown, records for the date of 9 December 1880 the marriage of William Burton Stewart, widower, of 73 Lower Clanham Street, occupation: Sorter GPO, father Henry Stuart, Sergeant, and Harriet Loftus Booth spinster, of Wilton Lodge Sandymount, occupation n/r, father George Loftus Booth, farmer.[30] The Loftus Booth family seem to have been farmers in north County Wicklow with a Sandymount connection as a grave record in that area reads:

A) George Loftus Booth Enniskerry Age 66 / May 1 1859
B) William Booth Kilcroney Cottage Son Of George Lofttus Booth Aged 28 / Dec 23 1854
C) Julia Booth Shore Bray Daughter Of George Loftus Booth Aged 7 / Aug 27th 1849
D) Jane Booth Wife Of George Loftus Booth Sandymount Age 76 / April 3rd 1878[31]

Sandymount started to grow around 1785 and building activities went on into the twenty-first century. Even after Pembroke Township ceased to exist as an independent local unit, significant ground was still owned by the Earl

Wilton Lodge, Claremont Road.

of Pembroke, who leased parts of the land to builders. These builders then sub-leased plots complete with houses on them for which the sub-tenant had to pay. Part of the Wilfield and Gilford area was developed in the early to mid-1930s. In an advertisement in *The Irish Times* of Saturday, 24 November 1935, houses in Wilfield Park were advertised for sale without mentioning a price. This together with the fact that the prospective buyer could choose his own site and could select from five different designs must have meant that those houses were not built yet. It is interesting to see that in this advertisement Willfield Park (still spelled with -ll-) is both described as 'Ballsbridge' and as '5 minutes from Ballsbridge'.

Those houses were often built in a similar style, with occasionally some slight differences from block to block. Modern planning permissions tend not to allow a change of style; even the railings of the front gardens should be kept in the same design. Pembroke Estate employed architects and engineers who made sure that their building specifications were kept meticulously.

Walking down Sandymount Avenue in 2013, the late Malachy Ryan of Wilfield Road reminisced, pointing to the houses on Gilford Road opposite the end of Sandymount Avenue:

This used to be much windier before they built those houses. The winds are tidal here. The tide changes twice a day and the wind changes with it.

Wilfield Road, off Sandymount Avenue. The houses were built in the early 1930s.

We used to live nearer the sea. In 1931 the family lived in Newgrove Avenue. It is not new anymore now, of course, it is nearly the oldest road in Sandymount.

Newgrove Avenue was developed in the 1820s:

The family lived there, in the third house from the sea. I was the baby then. There was hardly any traffic and they let me go down to the sea to play which was better than just having the front garden. Later the family decided to buy a house. Those houses down there were for renting, you rented them for a year or so. We went up and looked at the house but it was not a house yet, it was just the foundations.

The house he was talking about was built *c.* 1933. Arriving at the pet clinic shortly before Sandymount Green he pointed at it:

This here was all paddocks. They had ponies there, ponies and horses. Anyway I told the family were they going to spoil all the easy life, going down to the sea and all. But of course they did.

Sandymount today is nearly exclusively residential with shops, pubs and a few small firms. The biggest open spaces are the pitches of sport clubs of which there are quite a few in the village, often sharing their pitch with another club. Not much more than 100 years ago it was different; there still were sizeable areas without any buildings, and residences like Wilfield, Claremont, Lakelands and Roslyn Park were situated in big, park-like gardens.

Advertisement in *The Irish Times,* 24 November 1934.

ECONOMY

After the end of the early industries of brick-making and distilling, Sandymount became rural and residential. Even at the beginning of the twentieth century Sandymount was far more rural than it is today. According to the 1901 and 1911 censuses and the 1907 OS map some dairies existed still in Sandymount, of which one survived into the second half of the twentieth century. Those dairies had their own dairy cows. Quite often some members of those dairy families became butchers.

The area between the railway, Wilfield, Park Avenue and what the 1907 map describes as 'cricket field' was occupied by the Royal Nurseries. This area is now built up with houses in Park Lane, Park Court and Kirkwood. The old back entrance to the nurseries can still be found on Wilfield Road between Nos 57a and 59. This gap between different blocks of terraced houses has the width of a street in a residential area and is situated exactly opposite the end of Park Lane, but for some reason a wall blocks access to Park Lane from Wilfield Road.

The *Official Industrial Directory for Ireland*[32] lists some businesses in Sandymount in 1954. These are Francis J. McNally of 10 Newgrove Avenue, Sandymount, listed under 'Leather dog collars, leads, muzzles, etc.', the National Vaccination Institute, 80 Sandymount Road, who made medical and pharmaceutical preparations as well as vaccination packs; Richardson, Tee, Rycroft & Co. (Dublin), Ltd of 17 Gilford Road, Sandymount, who are listed as producers of cotton fabric (knitted) and of underwear, and lastly the firm Storys (Ireland) Ltd which produced thermal storage heaters in Willow Lodge, Park Avenue. Willow Lodge is not situated directly on Park Avenue but reached by a lane that also leads to the pavilion of the Railway Union sport clubs. None of these firms are there still, some have moved, others do not exist anymore.

Despite the fact that Sandymount is the youngest of the four coastal villages of Dublin 4 it has the widest range of shops and other businesses. It used to have a post office for more than 150 years. Unfortunately An Post closed Sandymount Post Office in 2015, and until a new place for a post office is found, Sandymount inhabitants are served by the post offices in Ballsbridge or Ringsend.

SPORT

Sport has always been part of Sandymount life. The oldest pitch in the whole area that was exclusively reserved for sport events was situated between Sandymount Road and the sea. It was first known as Army Grounds, then as the pitch of the medical school of the Catholic University and later either as Freebooters Ground or as Shelbourne Park Football Ground, as it appears on the 1907 OS map. It is most likely that this ground was used by the Sandymount Cricket Club and by the early Sandymount Rugby Club. Later it was the home pitch of the soccer clubs Freebooters FC, Shelbourne FC and Tritonville FC. It ceased to exist in the 1920s when the area was developed to built houses for soldiers who had fought in the First World War. Of the clubs mentioned, only Shelbourne FC still exists, but it is no longer based in Sandymount.

In modern times three pitches were established in Sandymount, but many more sports clubs appeared. On Claremont Road YMCA Hockey Club and YMCA Cricket Club share a pitch, as do Monkstown Rugby FC and Pembroke Cricket Club whose pitch is situated between Park Avenue and Wilfield Road. An even greater number of clubs use the area of Railway Union Sports Club, situated between Park Avenue and St John's Road. Those are the Railway Union clubs for bowling, cricket, hockey, rugby, soccer and tennis. The Railway Union Bowling Club shares its green with the Bank of Ireland Bowling Club.

Some of the clubs in Sandymount had special affiliations. Those are mentioned in the names with the two YMCA clubs and with the Railway Union clubs. Railway Union originally was called 'The Railway and Steampacket Companies Irish Athletic and Social Union' which describes the groups that formed its first members. Monkstown FC had connections with the military services as well as the Royal College of Surgeons in Ireland (RCSI) and Trinity College Medical School. When on 24 November 2016 the club unveiled a plaque commemorating the members killed during the First World War, the list of eighty members included six privates, two lance corporals, one corporal, one lance sergeant and two sergeants, while the other sixty-eight were all officers up to the rank of brigadier general. Ten of those eighty had been in the medical corps, one private, seven captains and a lieutenant colonel.

Apart from that the youngest sport enthusiasts are happy to kick a ball around Sandymount Green, under the watchful eyes of their proud parents, and young adults (and older people) have the promenade or – at low tide – the whole expanse of Sandymount Strand as an exercise ground.

TRAFFIC

Like its sister villages, Sandymount has its share of workmen's cottages. In the case of Sandymount these are connected with the railway and the trams. Just east of the railway line and officially in Ballsbridge townland as far as the houses are concerned, is a row of cottages built for railway workers. The townland border between Ballsbridge and Sandymount, however, runs in a north-west–south-east direction through private gardens, so that over half the garden of No. 1 is in Sandymount and the minor part in Ballsbridge. The Ballsbridge part of the gardens increases when going south until at No. 9 all the garden is in Ballsbridge. This just proves that townland borders no longer have the administrative function they had over 100 years ago.

The lane leading to those houses is called Railway Cottages. The sign giving the name of that lane is one of the very few on which the English version is written first, over the Irish version, which in itself contains a mistake. The sign reads:

Railway Cottages
Iostán an Iarróid
[The Irish line should read: *Iostán an Iarnróid*, of course.]

Railway cottages are not the only dwelling places connected with traffic. Horse-drawn trams started to run in Dublin from 1872 and one of the first lines ran from Nelson's Pillar to Sandymount Tower. Horse-drawn trams were usually double-deckers. On the Sandymount line one of the conductors' duties was to remind passengers on the upper deck to duck their heads when travelling under the rather low Bath Avenue Bridge. This gave rise to a saying attributed to Myles na gCopaleen (Flann O'Brien's column in *The Irish Times*) that 'the gentlemen on the upper deck of the No. 4 tram cannot but be struck by the stonework of Bath Avenue Bridge'. When the trams were later electrified, the Sandymount line was the last to be modernised. After electrification it only ever ran single-decker trams, because Bath Avenue Bridge was too low for electric double-decker tram cars.

The depot of the Sandymount line was in Gilford Road, just up from Sandymount Tower, which had been the terminus of the No. 4 tram from the beginning.

The gates of the depot have been partly bricked up, but on the footpath in front of them the tracks are still visible, leading into the nearer and taller part of the depot for the electric tram cars that required higher halls. The older depot for the horse-drawn cars can still be seen on the right through the wrought iron gates. Behind that depot the tram company had cottages built for the tram workers. The bigger house at the beginning of the terrace of cottages housed the inspector and his family.

When those cottages were built, their official address was Tramway Cottages with the addition of 'Sandymount' to differentiate them from the Tramway Cottages in Donnybrook. After the demise of the trams, the address became Gilford Terrace.

The railway was built decades before the trams, as a connection between the new asylum harbour in Kingstown (Dún Laoghaire) and Dublin. The first plan was to transport goods on boats, using a ship canal that would lead into Ringsend's Grand Canal Docks. This canal would have run past Sandymount more or less in the area where the railway line is now. This would have meant bridges instead of level crossings, possibly the only advantage. On the other hand canals that were built in Ireland in the nineteenth century definitely would be too narrow for a decent water transport possibility today. Luckily the railway won over the canal.

When the railway was built in 1834, it was soon regarded as the border between Ballsbridge and Sandymount, despite a possible different configuration of townland borders. The DART now stops at Sandymount, but this stop was not in service continuously since the beginning of the railway. It was in service during the years 1835–41, 1860–62, 1882–1901 and 1928–60[33] and then continuously since the introduction of the DART in 1984. Sandymount Station is only for DART trains. Commuter and intercity trains do not stop there.

Tramway
Cottages,
Gilford Terrace.

Sandymount DART station and level crossing.

An interesting snippet of railway history has been reported by William Richard Le Fanu, younger brother of the ghost story writer Joseph Sheridan Le Fanu, and a railway engineer who wrote in his memoirs:

> In the year 1845 came the railway mania. Prospectuses in hundreds appeared, holding out the most enticing inducements to the public to take shares. One line was to develop the resources of Ballyhooly, a miserable village in the county of Cork; another to promote and encourage the cockle trade at Sandymount, where there is a strand on which, at low water, may be seen a dozen old women gathering cockles.[34]

Sandymount should think itself lucky that nothing came of that suggestion, as the level crossings at Serpentine Avenue and Sandymount Avenue cause enough traffic disturbances, especially during rush hour, and the inhabitants would not wish for any more level crossings. As far as railway accidents were concerned, Le Fanu tells an anecdote which proves that it might not always have been the car driver who caused havoc at a level crossing.

> Father H ... told me that he had got into a second-class carriage one night by the last train leaving Dublin for Bray. Before the train started,

a woman, whose name he could not remember, but whom he recognized as a parishioner, came to the door and said, 'Father James, have you any objection to my coming in here?' 'Not the least,' said he. So in she came, and sat on the seat opposite to him. Off went the train at such a pace as he had never known before; it jumped and swayed from side to side. Father H … was naturally much alarmed. The woman, observing this, said to him, 'Don't be the least uneasy, Father James. Sure it's my Jim that's driving; and when he has a dhrop taken, it's him that can make her walk.'[35]

SCHOOLS

According to different authors Sandymount had quite a number of private schools in the nineteenth century. The one that survived longest and is still in existence is the school for girls that Barbara Verschoyle founded in Sandymount Avenue around 1830, run by the Religious Sisters of Charity. Later those sisters moved from Sandymount Avenue to Lakelands where their school merged with the former Carmelite Sisters' school. The school is still in Lakelands, now run by the parish as a national school for girls. The national school for boys was in the care of the parish from its foundation in 1878 and is still run by the parish.

Most of the schools mentioned in earlier publications do not exist anymore. The Sandymount Academical Institution was privately run in Sandymount Castle on Sandymount Green for a couple of decades around the turn of the nineteenth century, first as a Protestant boarding school for boys and later as a Protestant day school for girls. Earlier, also on Sandymount Green, was the school for girls run by the Misses Hepenstal. At the time of the Misses Hepenstal a Mr Breslin ran a boarding school for young gentlemen, first in Mountain View, a terrace of houses at the northern end of Sandymount Road, then in the centre of Sandymount, and later in Prospect House at Prospect Terrace. Altogether the *Almanac of Pettigrew & Oulton* mentions five private schools in Sandymount in 1834 and seven in 1847, on top of the School House at Sandymount Green which was erected in 1833.[36] This was probably used as a school run by the Church of Ireland Parish of St Mary's, Donnybrook.

This school house at the corner of Sandymount Green and Claremont Road was erected by subscription and is shown on the 1837 OS map, described as 'School Ho'. Around forty years later the same building is described in a map as 'Court Ho.' though at that date it was not used as a court. It had been used for some years by the Methodist Congregation for

Former School House of 1833, now the office of an estate agent.

worship, until Christ Church on Sandymount Green was erected in 1864. At some stage the building housed Miss Abbot's Ladies Academy, which was one of a number of private schools in Sandymount at the end of the nineteenth century (most of them for young ladies).[37] Later it was for a long time the post office and is shown as 'P.O.' on the 1907 OS map. It now houses an estate agent. D'Alton[38] mentions beside this school a savings bank and a lending library in Sandymount.

The map of the 1860s that showed the courthouse at 20 Sandymount Green, also showed a large building on Sandymount Avenue, halfway between the railway and Gilford Road, called The Cottage. On the map of the OS 1837 series this does not exist yet. The OS map of 1907 shows the same building in the same place, naming it St Brendan's. Christy Brown (1932–81), the author of the book *My Left Foot* intermittently went to St Brendan's School-Clinic in Sandymount where he met Dr Robert Collis. The site kept its connection with a specialised medical institution: Cerebral Palsy Ireland (CPI), which was started in 1948 by Dr Collis, who founded the school in 1952. In that year CPI changed its name to National Association for Cerebral Palsy and in 1953 this moved to St Brendan's School-Clinic in Sandymount. A couple of years later the building proved inadequate for its purpose. In the 1960s a new school was built which was soon no longer up to the new understanding of the illness and the needs of the sufferers of cerebral palsy. Finally the building that exists today was opened in 1999 by the then Minister for Health and Children, Brian Cowen TD.[39] This school now has a pre-school programme in which children with and without disabilities are educated together.

As far as secondary schools are concerned, three of them have to be mentioned, even though only one of them is left. Sandymount High School was a privately-owned and run school at the corner between the railway and the River Dodder. The school was non-denominational and co-educational and run by the Cannon family. The Roman Catholic clergy was oppposed to schools of this type and soon the then Archbishop of Dublin, John Charles McQuaid, had called in the Marist Fathers to build a secondary school in Sandymount. It is not clear if it was accidental or intentional that this school was built directly beside Sandymount High School. The effect was that Marian College kept on growing and Sandymount High School had to close in 1999.

Marian College at that stage was just for boys. Girls could go to Roslyn Park School, where the Sister of the Sacred Heart of Mary ran a secondary school from 1950 to 1982. For a number of years there was no secondary school for girls in Sandymount, but now Marian College also takes girls.

In autumn 2016 the Department of Education bought Roslyn Park from Enable Ireland and plans to erect buildings there to house the Shellybanks Educate Together primary school, that until then is housed in provisional accommodation. It is also planned that a second level school will be built in the same complex and it is expected that this will be for both girls and boys.

SANDYMOUNT ARTISTS

Probably the best known person born near Sandymount is William Butler Yeats, whose bust can be found in Sandymount Green. He was born in 5 Sandymount Avenue, in a terrace of houses then called George's Villas, which being west of the railway in the townland of Smotscourt should be regarded as situated in Ballsbridge. His bust in Sandymount Green was sculpted in 1921 by Dublin born artist Albert G. Power (1881–1945).

John Butler Yeats, painter and father of William, Jack, Robert and their sisters Susan Mary (Lily), Elizabeth Corbett (Lolly) and Jane Grace, had lived with his uncle Robert Corbett in Sandymount Castle for some time until he moved to 18 Madeley Terrace on Sandymount Road. After his marriage to Susan Pollexfen in 1863 he moved with her to George's Villas, Sandymount

Albert G. Power's bust of William
Butler Yeats on Sandymount
Green.

Avenue, where William B. Yeats was born. W.B. Yeats was baptised in
St Mary's, Donnybrook. In 1867 the family moved to London.

James Pearse, a sculptor who among other things created the original
communion railing and pulpit in the Star of the Sea church, lived from
1884 to 1890 with his family, including his well-known sons Patrick and
William, in Newbridge Avenue, which forms the border between Irishtown
and Sandymount. Before that they had lived above the shop in 27 Great
Brunswick Street (now Pearse Street). In the last years of the nineteenth
century the Pearse family lived in the terrace called George's Villas on
Sandymount Avenue in the Ballsbridge part of this road. When James died
in 1900 they had to find something smaller and Mrs Pearse and her children
moved to 1 Lísreaghan Terrace (now No. 107 Sandymount Avenue, at the
corner with Gilford Road) in Sandymount.

As far as literature is concerned, Yeats is not the only famous name
connected with Sandymount. A house on Dromard Avenue, at some stage
called Seaford Avenue West, shows a plaque at first floor height, explaining
that James Joyce stayed there on 16 June 1904, the day described in his
novel *Ulysses*.

Some people insist that this is not quite right, as Joyce stayed in
Sandymount on 16 June 1904, but not in this house. He is supposed to have
stayed in this house, but in September 1904. On the other hand it is known

that the poet and playwright James Henry Sproule Cousins, who at that time lived in this house with his wife Gretta, had invited Joyce to stay with them for exactly that night.

Both Joyces, father and son, were great movers and there are at least three more places in Pembroke Urban District where James Joyce stayed, of which two are in Sandymount: 35 Strand Road and 103 Strand Road (the third address is 60 Shelbourne Road, in Ballsbridge).

Another writer from Sandymount was Annie Mary Patricia Smithson (1873–1948), an Irish novelist, poet and Nationalist, who was born into a Protestant family in Claremont Road. She was christened Margaret Anne Jane, but took the names Anne Mary Patricia on her conversion to Catholicism in 1907.

Valentin Iremonger (1918–91) was also born in Sandymount. He was a diplomat, but also a poet and many of his poems are set in Sandymount.

One writer from the area seems to be long forgotten. *The Irish Times* of Monday, 15 August 2011 described a poetic competition that the same paper had organised in 1887, asking their lady readers to write a poem in praise of the golden jubilee of Queen Victoria. The prize was won by Augusta H. Lover of 21 Sandymount Green, with a poem, the opening lines of which ran:

> Hark! An anthem slowly swelling
> Echoes far o'er land and sea,
> 'Tis a year of joy and gladness,
> 'Tis Victoria's jubilee …

ARTWORK

Besides the bust of W.B. Yeats on Sandymount Green there are a few more public sculptures in Sandymount. Opposite the bust of Yeats on Sandymount Green and facing him across the lawn a bust of Séamus Justin Heaney by Carolyn Mulholland was erected in June 2016. Heaney had lived the last years of his life in Merrion, but during this time he himself always insisted that he lived in Sandymount.

Not on, but very near Sandymount Green is a female nude figure, which stands in front of an office building that once housed a section of the Revenue – the corporate tax office for County Wicklow.

Another sculpture can be found in front of Sandymount Hotel (formerly Mount Herbert Hotel). This one is called 'Sandymount Line-Out' and was

Above: The bust of Séamus Heaney (1939–2013) on Sandymount Green.

Above right: Statue on Claremont Road.

Right: 'Sandymount Line-Out'.

commissioned in 2010 by John Loughran, owner of Sandymount Hotel and a great rugby fan, to celebrate the return of rugby to Lansdowne Road in 2010 after the opening of the AVIVA Stadium. The statue was sculpted by DS Art in Beijing.

Very near this statue, at the end of Herbert Road near Marian College and the Dodder which forms the border to Irishtown, the oldest Sandymount letterbox is found, which is of a rather uncommon type: a big Victorian wall box, more than double the size of the usual wall letterbox. It is not strictly a work of art, but definitely a rarity.

The two monumental statues on Sandymount Strand will be mentioned in the chapter describing a walk along the coast.

SANDYMOUNT PEOPLE

Some people from Sandymount still remember well-known actors who lived in the neighbourhood. One of them was Noel Purcell, who for many years lived in Wilfield Road. Another twentieth-century actor who lived in Sandymount was Arthur Shields. There was also Anew McMaster who lived on Strand Road in a house that his brother-in-law, Micheál MacLiammóir, shared with him for some time.

Sandymount has many connections with writers. Literature, however, is not the only art form represented in the village. The musician John Steward Beckett (1927–2007), a first cousin of the writer Samuel Beckett, was born in Sandymount. The composer J.S. Beckett was also a choir conductor and brilliant harpsichordist. He was interested in medieval and Renaissance music and loved Johann Sebastian Bach, whose cantatas he directed in St Ann's, Dawson Street, on Sunday afternoons every February from 1972 to 1981. When in 1979 a choir and orchestra from the Republic of Ireland was for the first time invited to the Proms in the Royal Albert Hall in London, Beckett was the conductor. John F. Larchet, Professor of Music at UCD, and for decades director of music at the Abbey Theatre and President and Musical Director of the Dublin Grand Opera Society, also was born in Sandymount.

Some painters who lived in Sandymount deserve a mention, though not all of them were famous for their work. William Bourke Kirwan, a miniature painter who was born around 1814 was better known because of a trial in which he was condemned to death for the supposed murder of his wife. He was suspected partly because he had 'maintained a separate establishment at Sandymount, where he had a mistress by whom he had eight children'.

As the evidence was not conclusive, his sentence was later commuted to transportation for life.[40]

William Ashford has been mentioned in connection with the House with the Eggcup on Top (Roslyn Park). He was born in Birmingham in 1746 and came to Dublin in 1764. He became a well-known landscape painter who worked exclusively in Ireland and painted a series of pictures of Mount Merrion, the Irish seat of the Fitzwilliam and later the Herbert family.

Ashford was a founding member and the first elected President of the Royal Hibernian Academy (RHA). He died in Sandymount on 17 April 1824. Another painter and founding member of the Royal Hibernian Academy and its first keeper was Thomas James Mulvany, who for part of his life lived in Sandymount, even though his exact address is unknown. Data about him might have been kept in Academy House, the purpose-built home of the RHA, which was destroyed by fire during the Easter Rising of 1916, when all the earlier records of the Academy were lost.

Thomas James's family later moved to Booterstown. The second of his sons, George Francis Mulvany, was a painter like his father and another keeper of the Royal Hibernian Academy. He had campaigned a long time for the foundation of a National Gallery of Ireland and when this finally was founded, he became its first director. He was possibly born in Sandymount before the family moved to Booterstown. Both he and his father Thomas attended the Drawing School of the Dublin Society (now known as the Royal Dublin Society (RDS)). Also well known is his younger brother John Skipton Mulvany who was an architect and built many railway stations, including Broadstone Station, Dún Laoghaire, Monkstown and Salthill, Blackrock, and Dalkey railway stations, as well as railway stations in Galway, Ballinasloe, Moate and Athlone. He was also the architect for the Royal St George Yacht Club in Dún Laoghaire.

The eldest son of Thomas James, William Thomas Mulvany, was definitely born in Sandymount. He entered the civil service and worked his way up to become Commissioner of the Board of Public Works. After some disputes with the House of Lords he retired from the civil service and afterwards moved to Germany, where he was influential in developing the western part of the Ruhr Valley industrial area.

In an article in *The Irish Times* in the weekend edition of Saturday, 5 June 2005, Derek Scally called him 'Irish King of the Ruhr'. The German town of Gelsenkirchen of now 260,000 inhabitants awarded William Thomas Mulvany the freedom of the city in 1865. Streets are named after him in the German cities and towns of Düsseldorf, Gelsenkirchen, Herne and Castrop-Rauxel and – what is possibly more important for an

Left: Thomas James Mulvany (1779–1845) painted by his son George Francis Mulvany.

Right: William Thomas Mulvany (b. 11 March 1806, Sandymount, d. 30 October 1884, Düsseldorf). (Xylography by Richard Brend'amour)

Irishman – there was even a beer named after him. A great-grandson of his (Dr Hans-Christoph Seebohm) was West German Federal Minister for Traffic for seventeen years and used to wear a golden shamrock in his lapel in memory of his Irish forebears. A great-great-grandson became a professor of philosophy. His full name was Professor William Thomas Mulvany Seebohm. His German descendants and the area he helped to develop honour the memory of William Thomas Mulvany. In his birthplace of Sandymount, however, few people know about him.

As far as politicians are concerned, James Stephens, the Fenian, should be mentioned. He lived for some months in Fairfield House at the corner of Newbridge Avenue and Herbert Road where he was arrested in 1865. Éamon de Valera stayed in 18 Claremont Road for a while in a house where his wife Sinéad had lived while Éamon was in Arbour Hill Prison and where they were re-united after his release in 1924.

Some clerical gentlemen should perhaps be mentioned as well. Revd Fletcher Sheridan Le Fanu (1860–1939), son of the railway engineer Richard William Le Fanu and nephew of the writer Joseph Sheridan Le Fanu[41] was rector of St John the Evangelist in Sandymount and according to the censuses of 1901 and 1911 lived in the vicarage at the border between Sandymount and Merrion.

Revd Tresham Dames Gregg, born in Dublin in 1801, was ordained a priest in the Archdiocese of York, came back to Ireland and as curate of Swift Alley Church became a celebrated preacher. He was so strongly anti-Catholic that the then Archbishop of Dublin forbade him to preach in the archdiocese of Dublin. He was known as 'Thrash'em Gregg', wrote many books and lived in Sandymount for many years. Later in life he became very strange in his ideas and was convinced that a divine disclosure in 1866 had told him that he was immortal. Despite this conviction he died in obscurity in 55 Strand Road, Sandymount, on 28 October 1881.[42]

5

MERRION

The four sister villages are not described according to their age, as is usual for sisters. They are described geographically from north to south, and so Merrion is last, despite the fact that according to the generally accepted timeline it is older than any of the others. That sometimes there is confusion about Merrion is to some extent caused by the move of Richard, Fifth Viscount Fitzwilliam of Merrion from the dilapidated Merrion Castle in the townland Merrion in Pembroke, parish of Donnybrook, barony of Dublin, to Merrion House in Mount Merrion in the townland of Merrion, parish of Taney (Dundrum), barony of Rathdown. Since then the original Merrion on the coast is often referred to as Old Merrion.

The name Merrion is difficult to explain. In his introduction to Booterstown, Nicholas Donnelly mentions the old name Tracht Fuirbthen for a part of the coast on the southern part of Dublin Bay, stretching from Sandymount to Blackrock. This Fuirbthen changed to Muirbthen in Middle Irish and finally to Muirbhthean in modern Irish, where it sounds very much like names for this area quoted in Anglo-Norman documents which could be Muryong or Myryonge and variations thereof, until finally the name settled as Merrion.[1]

MERRION AND THE PALE

The Pale was the area of the east coast under Norman and later English rule. The word originally stands for the border of this area (from Latin '*palus*', meaning stake or border post – a word that also is used in 'palisade' and 'paling'). Some parts of the Pale in this latter sense as border have survived as a double ditch with a pathway. For the defence of the Pale, and especially its borders, tower houses were built from the thirteenth century onwards. Thorncastle in Williamstown and Merrion Castle were two of those defensive structures. Both were changed over the course of centuries and finally both became ruined and now have disappeared completely.

Merrion Castle was first mentioned in 1334 as the property of Thomas Bagod who already owned the castle of Baggotrath. The latter had been built by him around 1280 and Merrion Castle might be of similar age. The castle is later mentioned in an Act of 1488 that describes the boundary of the Pale.[2] The village of that name can be regarded as contemporary with the castles, considering that the castle was surrounded by stables, gardens and fields, needing people to work them and these people had to be housed. Built as a fortification against the 'Wild Irish' Merrion Castle certainly would have accommodated soldiers in or near it.

The name Merrion appears in old texts in different variations: 'Myrrionge', 'Mirryonge', 'Mirryyong', 'Meryong' and 'Meryon'. Those various forms are mentioned in documents from the fifteenth century onwards and it is possible that the name originally was given to the whole coast of this area; Dinneen translates 'Muirbhthean' as 'Seashore' but also as 'Merrion, near Dublin'.[3]

Merrion Castle changed owners quite a few times in the first century or so of its existence until it came into the ownership of the Fitzwilliam family at the end of the fourteenth century.[4] Excavations found metal tools used for carpentry and horse shoeing as well as pottery in the area near it. This and carbon dating show that the first castle was inhabited from the late thirteenth to the early fifteenth century.

The medieval castle was later re-erected in the style of a manor house. F. Elrington Ball imagined it in the sixteenth century as a stately building in the middle of gardens and orchards and fields of corn. According to Ball, Monkstown Castle and Simmonscourt Castle would have been the nearest neighbours.

Merrion Castle and Elm Park House. (C. Conroy)

The picture above shows Merrion Castle as depicted in a booklet by C. Conroy, who quotes Ball as his source. Ball's publication shows as Merrion Castle a building that Conroy describes as 'Elm Park House c. 1755'.

What Conroy describes as Merrion Castle Ball mentions as 'Spranger Barry's House'. Ball then says about the drawing of Merrion Castle in his *Historical Sketch* 'owing to defective perspective the original connection of the imposing staircase and of the two fortified buildings, which the drawing depicts …'.[5]

Perhaps he mixed up the drawings, as his description of Merrion Castle does not suit the drawing that he describes as Merrion Castle.

Gaskin mentions that Sir Simon Harcourt was shot in an attempt to get Carrickmines from the Irish in 1642. He was brought to Merrion and died there 'at the house of Lord Fitzwilliam'.[6] This Fitzwilliam was Sir Thomas Fitzwilliam, First Viscount Fitzwilliam of Merrion and Baron Fitzwilliam of Thorncastle. He was born in 1581 and succeeded his father as head of the family in 1595. He was elevated to the rank of viscount in 1629 and died in 1650.

A drawing of Merrion Castle by Gabriel Beranger, published in 1766 and kept in the National Library of Ireland shows a ruin with crenellated outside walls which could much better be correlated with the drawing shown as Merrion Castle by Conroy than the one Ball calls Merrion Castle, as this latter one does not have crenellated walls.

MERRION FROM AROUND 1700

The village around the castle remained small. The castle was situated in the parish of Booterstown, in the area that is now occupied by the Caritas Centre of the Religious Sisters of Charity (formerly St Mary's Centre for the Visually Impaired). In 1686 the landlord of this area, Thomas, Fourth Viscount Fitzwilliam, built a chapel for the villagers in Booterstown, but there seems to have been an older chapel and graveyard nearer the castle. Conroy says in his *Historic Merrion*[7] that the graveyard was first used in 1300 and that it originally was bigger and reached to the Rock Road. The chapel there was mentioned in the will of Richard Fitzwilliam who died in 1528. This chapel has completely disappeared. Richard Lewis had seen the ruins of it in the late eighteenth century as he reports: 'OLD MERRION. A small village, two miles and a half from the Castle of Dublin, where there are ruins of an old Church and Castle.'[8]

The graveyard is still accessible, just off the Rock Road on Bellevue Avenue, between a petrol station and the Tara Towers Hotel car park. Its little gate is easily overlooked in this narrow cul-de-sac. The huge iron bolt is not locked. The graveyard was closed for burials in 1866. Now it is a peaceful little place unknown to most people.

This graveyard contains a headstone commemorating the soldiers who lost their lives when the packet boat *Prince of Wales* was wrecked near Blackrock and the *Rochdale* near Seapoint in fog and a fierce easterly gale in 1807, a tragedy that initiated the plans for Dún Laoghaire Harbour as asylum harbour for ships in similar difficulties.

The inscription which is not fully legible anymore is quoted in Revd Beaver H. Blacker's *Brief Sketches of the Parishes of Booterstown and Donnybrook*:

> Sacred to the memory of the soldiers belonging to His Majesty's 18th Regiment of Foot, and a few belonging to other corps, who, actuated by the desire of more extensive service, nobly volunteered from the South Mayo and different Regiments of Irish Militia into the line and who were unfortunately shipwrecked on this coast in the Prince of Wales Packet, and perished on the night of the 19th of November, 1807. This tribute to their memory has been placed on their tomb by order of General the Earl of Harrington, Commander of the Forces in Ireland.[9]

The village might not have been big then, but it was well enough known by Dublin citizens as in 1837 S. Lewis wrote about Merrion:

> Here are several neat villas occupied during the summer months by visitors resorting hither for the benefit of sea-bathing, for which purpose the fine broad and firm strand at this place is well adapted.[10]

The same author mentions Elm Park, Bloomfield, Merrion Castle and Merrion Hall as the principal seats, explaining that 'Merrion Castle' got its name from the ivied ruins of the old castle. A few years later (1841) Merrion had a population of 523 people who lived in seventy-two houses[11]. Revd Beaver H. Blacker quotes the 1851 census, according to which Merrion had 725 inhabitants and an area of 197 acres, compared to Sandymount which had 1419 inhabitants on 243 acres.[12] The increase of nearly 40 per cent in the population within only ten years can perhaps be explained by different times of the year in which the census was taken, as according to Lewis some villas were occupied only in summer, so a census at that time would give a higher number of inhabitants than one conducted in winter.

Clean air, proximity of the sea and good transport facilities by railway and tram made the area not only attractive for summer residences in the late

The convent of the
Religious Sisters of
Charity (from an old
postcard, *c.* 1900).

The old entrance to
St Mary's, Merrion.

nineteenth century, but also for institutions involved in care. In the mid-1860s the Religious Sisters of Charity bought Merrion Castle for £2,000.

In 1868 the sisters opened St Mary's Home and School for the Female Blind there and from 1872 they ran St Martha's Industrial School for Females in the same grounds. By 1882 this was one of the largest industrial schools for girls in Ireland with around 150 girls aged eight to twelve years.

St Mary's went from an asylum for the female blind to a centre for the visually impaired. The chapel was built in 1880. St Martha's Industrial School was closed in 1919. Lately more housing units have been built there and the complex now includes the Caritas Rehabilitation Centre. With this development the old entrance on Rock Road was closed, as it was too narrow and new ways to enter and leave the complex were opened a bit further south on Rock Road (for emergencies) and from Elm Park Apartments.

A bit further north from this centre and on the other side of Merrion Road, St John's House of Rest was founded in 1869, originally in a very small house, 'where men, women and children in poor psychological and physical health were offered temporary rest, spiritual renewal and a change of diet'.[13] It was enlarged in 1880 and is still a nursing home, situated between the Merrion Inn and the Merrion Parish Church of Our Lady of Peace.

The centre of today's Merrion village.

MERRION TODAY

During the last 200 years the village of Merrion has moved slightly to the north-west, with a row of shops just south of the twentieth-century parish church and opposite the private section of St Vincent's Hospital. There is also a bank and a restaurant.

Despite being the oldest of the 'Four Sisters' – the coastal villages of Dublin 4 – Merrion looks least like a village, but on the other hand it has the most traffic of all. Just opposite the old entrance of St Mary's, Merrion's three main traffic arteries come together at Merrion Gates: Strand Road, Merrion Road and the railway. This is the reason why such a small village has four petrol stations, one on Strand Road and three on Merrion Road. For over thirty years there is also a company selling and maintaining cars.

Apart from the small shops on Merrion Road, Merrion Shopping Centre at the corner of Merrion Road and Nutley Lane has a further collection of shops and cafés, including a barber, a butcher, a chemist, a photo shop, shops for clothes, leatherware and jewellery, besides a hardware shop and a big newsagent cum stationer. Together with a big supermarket they fill the ground floor of the building that in its upper floor has offices for a big insurance company and the Embassy of Japan.

On Strand Road a modernist building with the name of Merrion Hall (originally the headquarters of Córas Tráchtála) stands on the site of the former residence with that name. It is now an office block which also includes a Montessori school.

The Coach and Horses Inn of the nineteenth century was located opposite Merrion Gates. It was bought by the Sisters of Charity and in 1995 taken down for the enlargement of the facilities of St Mary's. Until the end of the nineteenth century the Rock Road was notorious for highwaymen and robberies and the Coach & Horses Inn suffered as well. J. Joyce reports that in 1807 it was 'attended' by a number of highwaymen who relieved the proprietor of £60, which was an enormous sum at that time. Joyce goes on:

> They then adjourned to the bar parlour, where they remained for about an hour drinking, and the health of the host was proposed and drunk with much enthusiasm, after which the unbidden guests departed with many apologies for their intrusion.[14]

Don't let anybody say that the Irish are not polite, even when they are highwaymen!

The Merrion Inn, 2010.

Merrion still has an inn, the Merrion Inn which is situated further north from where the Coach and Horses Inn had been, and on the other side of the road. It is not certain how long this site has been occupied by an inn. The 1837 OS map shows a building in this site that is rather narrow, its long side facing the road with enough room in front for carriages to stop. On the 1907 OS map the building is enlarged to the back, though the front still looks like the older building of 1837. In 1907 it was called Merrion House. The 1901 and 1911 censuses do not mention a public house in this area. The Merrion Inn as it stands today was refurbished in 1991 by the family who took it over that year. In June 2012 it was damaged by fire which was attended by five units of Dublin Fire Brigade for six or seven hours. This was partly precautionary, as the next door neighbour of Merrion Inn on its south side is a petrol station.

Nobody was hurt, but the roof was completely destroyed. The fire damaged the first floor considerably and the ground floor was damaged by water during the efforts of the Dublin Fire Brigade. The Inn was restored and is still in business in 2017.

Fire seems to be the lesser problem in Merrion, with water being a bigger threat. Not the lack of it, quite the contrary. This is not only because at very

Pump House, Ailesbury Gardens.

high tides the sea tends to flood Strand Road, coming in from the strand at Merrion Gates. This does not concern the houses on the sea side of Strand Road as they seem to be built on a slight ridge, while the ground on the land side of Strand Road is noticeably lower and more prone to flooding. Old maps show lots of small and bigger pools in the area. The 1837 OS map shows a lake or lagoon between the railway and the sea. Nowadays this area has been developed and many of the houses in St Alban's Park, Martello Views and Merrion Strand are built where this lake used to be. The ground water level in the area is constantly checked and – if necessary – lowered by pumps in a rather unobtrusive little house near the railway line in Ailesbury Gardens opposite the junction with St Alban's Park that looks like a garden shed.

To make quite sure that nobody tries to break into this 'garden shed' it has a notice over its door:

Baile Átha Cliath

Seirbhísi Fuíolluisce

Tá an forgneamh seo ina

chuid rithábhachtach den

chóras draenála

i gcás éigeandála

glaoigh ar

01 6683886

Dublin City

Wastewater Services

These premises are a vital

part of the drainage system

In emergency

please call

01 6683886

RESIDENCES

Two houses on Sydney Parade are interesting because of their ages and their names. Perhaps they are two of the dwellings that S. Lewis[15] included in the

Herbert Lodge,
53 Sydney
Parade.

Ailesbury House.

'neat villas' that he mentioned. They are Pembroke Lodge and its neighbour Herbert Lodge.

These buildings are older than St John's Church, as they are both shown on the 1837 OS map with the same names that they still have which points to a connection with the Pembroke Estate of the Herbert family. Not far from them, on the other (north) side of Sydney Parade Avenue was a house of which only the road sign is left, commemorating it among a small estate of much more modern residences: Páirc Richelieu/Richelieu Park. The 1907 OS map shows the house with this name, standing in its own little park. On the earlier OS map of 1837 the name of the house is Rich View.

The nearby Ailesbury House at the corner of Ailesbury Road with Merrion Road was the residence of the miller and baker William O'Brien (of Johnston, Mooney and O'Brien).

It is younger than the residences mentioned by S. Lewis. Even the OS map of 1865 does not show yet. Today it is the residence of the Spanish Ambassador. The chancellery of the Spanish Embassy on Merlin Park is behind the garden of Ailesbury House on the border between Merrion and Ballsbridge townlands. Also in the former grounds of Ailesbury House is the building that houses the Embassy of the Netherlands, fronting Merrion Road.

Embassy of the Netherlands.

Rockville House, formerly Williamstadt.

The lamp post in front of the Dutch Embassy shows in its construction that it started life as one of the posts holding up the overhead electric wires for the former tram system. Altogether Merrion houses four embassies. The third after the Spanish and the Dutch Embassy is that of Pakistan, nearly opposite the residence of the Spanish Ambassador on Ailesbury Road and the fourth is that of Japan at the corner of Nutley Lane and Merrion Road, a site which many would describe as Ballsbridge, despite its name; Merrion Shopping Centre.

Another Victorian residence occupies the corner between Sydney Parade Avenue and Ailesbury Road. The late Victorian building is mentioned with the name Williamstadt on the 1907 OS map and with the same name in Thom's Directory in 1930. It is now called Rockville House.

Sydney Parade Avenue is shown on the 1837 OS map as Sydney Parade, which had very few houses then. There are some small buildings between Herbert Lodge and Pembroke Lodge and Strand Road and on the other side the 1837 map shows the gate lodge for Rich View as well as a bigger building called Merrion Lodge at the corner with Merrion Road. The 1907 OS still shows free spaces, though there are more houses, mostly from the late Victorian and Edwardian period.

St Vincent's University Hospital.

ST VINCENT'S HOSPITAL

All the residences mentioned by S. Lewis have disappeared, but of one of them the gate is still there, even giving its name 'Bloomfield' on the outside.

Old maps show that this gate on Merrion Road stood in front of a drive which was so long that the house it led to was not in Merrion townland, but in a townland called Priesthouse to the south-west of Merrion. Priesthouse never belonged to Pembroke Township as it was situated in the half-barony of Rathdown. Of the other residences Lewis mentions for Merrion, the original Elm Park was just inside Merrion townland whereas Nutley was in Priesthouse townland. Merrion Castle and Merrion Hall were always in Merrion.

Seen from the other side the gate that in the 1907 OS map is still marked 'Bloomfield Entrance' today looks as if it is at the beginning of a long lane through an estate with shrubs and trees. The mansion itself has long gone and the gate is always locked as it no longer functions as an entrance.

What is behind it now is St Vincent's University Hospital, the biggest employer in the area.

St Vincent's Hospital was not in Elm Park from the beginning. It was founded by Mother Mary Aikenhead in 1835 on St Stephen's Green and moved to Elm Park only in 1970. Since 1999 its official name is St Vincent's University Hospital (SVUH) as it is attached to University College Dublin. About ten years ago the hospital was rebuilt. A yearbook of 1850 describes the old hospital in the city centre:

ST. VINCENT'S HOSPITAL AND DISPENSARY
STEPHEN'S GREEN EAST

This noble Institution was opened in 1835, by the Sisters of Charity, with the concurrence of their founder, the Most Revd Dr. Murray, Catholic Archbishop of Dublin. The Hospital contains 80 beds, constantly occupied by cases of great urgency, and has attached to it a Dispensary, where great numbers of sick are relieved. Both are open to the afflicted without any regard to religious distinctions. The plans and economy of the Hospital are modelled on those of the great Hospitals la Petite Enfans Malades, &c., of Paris, for which purpose some of the Sisters have been for a considerable time residing in those establishments abroad.

Its funds are derived from voluntary subscriptions, donations, bequests, and an annual charity sermon, recognised by the Colleges of Surgeons in Dublin and London, the London University, &c.[16]

St Vincent's has had a good reputation from the beginning and it carries on the ethos of the Sisters of Charity who still own it, even though the hospital nurses are no longer members of that religious order.

TOURISM

Merrion Railway Station was built in 1834 and opened in 1835, but as at that stage there were not so many houses in the area one might wonder about the reason for a station there. Perhaps it was built because the railway chairman of that time lived in Merrion Castle nearby.[17] The station was closed in 1929; trains do not stop there anymore and the platforms have disappeared. The old station building, however, still exists and is now used as a dwelling place.

Merrion Baths and its pier. (From Colin Conroy, *Historic Merrion*)

From 1879 on the railway had competition in the form of trams. Merrion was traversed by lines 6 (to Blackrock), 7 (to Kingstown/Dún Laoghaire) and 8 (to Dalkey). Those lines were the first to be electrified in 1896. Line No. 8, the Dalkey line, was the last one running. When the older tram era in Dublin stopped on Saturday, 9 July 1949, the last No. 8 tram left Nelson's Pillar to arrive in Dalkey in a very dilapidated state due to souvenir hunters who dismantled the tram.

Merrion Strand is the southernmost strand in the Dublin City part of Dublin Bay. The OS map of 1837 shows a bath on Merrion Strand, opposite Merrion Gates, which was still there in the OS map of 1865, but it closed at the end of the nineteenth century. These baths were further south and obviously some decades older than the Merrion Baths whose remains are still in situ today. Some baths in this area were built and run by the railway company.

Not far from the Martello Tower are the remains of the later Merrion Baths, at high tide often surrounded by water. Those baths were originally connected with the shore by a pier that reached Strand Road south of the tower opposite the modern petrol station. Both pier and baths were opened on 28 July 1883 and had to be demolished in the 1920s as they had deteriorated enormously. They were later than Cranfield's Baths in Irishtown and lasted some decades longer.

Last remains of the entrance to Merrion Bath.

Only one small part of the pier or rather the entrance to it is left today: a brick quoin of the entrance gate on Strand Road, now incorporated into the sea wall.

What remains of the bath itself is loved by graffiti artists. Dublin City Council is not pleased with the work of those 'artists', however, and keeps repainting the remains of the baths in a very dull grey or beige. Not that that helps much, as the graffiti people seem to like the idea that they are regularly provided with a fresh canvas for new ideas.

Lately a conservation report found the Merrion Baths to be in such a ruinous and dangerous state that it recommended a partial or even complete demolition.[18]

RELIGIOUS BUILDING

The townland border between Merrion and Sandymount is St John's Road and follows the southern part of this street around the church so that the church itself is officially in Sandymount. The Parochial Hall, however, on the south side of the church and the street, clearly is on Merrion townland.

This Parochial Hall was sold in 1962 to Patrick Joseph Duffy who in 1952 had founded Salle d'Armes Duffy as well as the Irish Academy of Arms (Académie d'Armes d'Irlande). From 1962 on he used the former parish hall as a fencing school. The sign is still at the gate though the fencing school was closed in 2005.

Former Parochial Hall of St John the Evangelist.

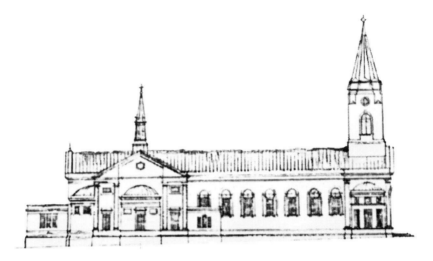

Architect's drawing for a church in Merrion (1950). (Drawing 9/05/50 in archives of parish church reproduced in Colin Conroy, *Historic Merrion*)

Church of Our Lady, Queen of Peace, Merrion.

In 1925 the building of a Roman Catholic church in Merrion was considered, as the chapel in the old graveyard had long disappeared but the number of inhabitants of Merrion had grown. Plans for this proposed church were drawn and published, but the plan was not executed. In 1940 a chapel of ease, a plain wooden structure was erected at the site where the church is now. Ten years later the idea of a church was taken up again and an architect's drawing of it has survived.

Finally, in 1955, a church was opened, built after plans approved by John Charles McQuaid, Archbishop of Dublin. In 1964 it became the Merrion Parish Church of Our Lady, Queen of Peace.

Like many churches built around the middle of the twentieth century, the side facing the road is much more ornate than the rest. This usually is not noticed, as most of those churches are either surrounded by houses or by trees. Not so in Merrion, where the church has a thoroughfare on its west side and a big car park south-east of it, which leaves the view of the long and unadorned east side in full view. The northern end of the church is not particularly interesting either. However, not many people see the northern end of the church, as the footpath beside and the footbridge across the railway line are less in use than they were in earlier years when people walked to church instead of driving there. Passengers in the DART might get a short glimpse of it, but will not have time enough to study the building when passing. Churches traditionally are built with the entrance in the west and the altar in the east. This church has the entrance in the south and the altar in the north.

Merrion occasionally features in radio reports, usually in the traffic news, as the Merrion Road–Rock Road stretch can be quite congested during rush hour and if there is an incident at Merrion Gates level crossing, the trains are affected as well.

AGRICULTURE AND INDUSTRY

Merrion, like its northern neighbours Sandymount and Ballsbridge, had agricultural areas and nurseries before the land was developed for housing. S. Lewis mentions the 'extensive nursery grounds of Messrs Simpson as being 'in the vicinity' after listing Merrion residences. According to the OS map of 1837 those nurseries were in the Nutley Lane, Nutley Avenue and Nutley Road area in Priesthouse townland and should be counted to Donnybrook, and not to Merrion. Some 100 years later, however, there was still land in Merrion that could be used for agriculture. In 1935 Dublin Corporation presented the Mount Street Club with two allotments along the railway line, a one-acre plot, described as 'at Sydney Parade' and a three-acre plot described as 'at Merrion'. Both of those plots are on Merrion townland. It was not the best land for agricultural purposes, as it was badly drained and full of weeds and rushes.

The members of Mount Street Club were not discouraged and put an enormous effort into their plots as in 1938 the same source reports that the plots produced '18 tons of potatoes, along with a vast amount of cabbages, and lesser crops, including 200 bunches of carrots, 6 hundredweight of turnips, celery, leeks, broccoli, cauliflower and pickling cabbage.'[19]

As far as industry is concerned, Merrion had the Invisible Mending and Cleaning Company (IMCO) works, built in 1930. This firm had its headquarters in Grafton Street and up to seven shops in Dublin, which sent clothes to the Merrion works for cleaning and mending.[20] The Merrion works were extended in 1932, 1938, 1949 and 1955–57.[21]

The firm had to close its works in Merrion in 1973 after more and more individual dry cleaners appeared that had on-site cleaning facilities. The building itself was demolished and an office block was erected on the site in 1975.

MERRION INHABITANTS

Merrion Castle was the seat of the Fitzwilliam family from around 1550 until 1710. The Fitzwilliams were the landlords of the area. At the end of the nineteenth century the miller and baker William O'Brien (of the firm Johnston, Mooney and O'Brien) lived in Ailesbury House at the corner of Ailesbury Road and Merrion Road (now the residence of the Spanish Ambassador). Sir Thomas ffrench, Fourth baron ffrench had Elm Park as one of his residences in the end of the nineteenth century. In 1920 Éamon de Valera occasionally used 165 Strand Road as a hiding place. General Emmet Dalton, one of the organisers of the Irish Free State Army, eyewitness of the murder of Michael Collins and founder of the Ardmore Film Studios in Bray died in Sydney Parade. The actor and comedian James Augustus (Jimmy) O'Dea ('Mrs Biddy Mulligan, the Pride of the Coombe') lived in Herbert Avenue in the 1930s. Séamus Heaney, Nobel Laureate for Poetry, lived in Strand Road, near the Merrion Gates, from 1976 until his death in 2013. He always said that he lived in Sandymount.

A WALK ALONG THE COAST

Flying into Dublin often provides a good view of nearly the whole of Dublin Bay from the air.

On the ground a good point to see most of the coast of Dublin 4 with Irishtown, Sandymount and Merrion Strands is from the green path on the south side of the Poolbeg Peninsula.

Walking along the Dublin 4 seashore from Poolbeg Lighthouse to Merrion Gates is very pleasant, as long as the weather is dry. To walk the whole stretch (around 6.5km or 4 miles) would take between an hour and a half and two hours' walking time, not counting time for any stops.

Dublin Bay, looking south.

THE GREAT SOUTH WALL AND IRISHTOWN
NATURE PARK

The first couple of kilometres on that walk are not along a strand but on an artificial structure: the Great South Wall, one of the longest sea walls in Europe and of those long ones probably the oldest. It was built between 1716 and 1795 and is around 6km long. The length seems less now after the reclamation of the land that forms the Poolbeg Peninsula. On the first kilometre, starting from the lighthouse, there is water on either side of the wall, even at low tide. At high tide another kilometre has water on either side.

The first kilometre of the Great South Wall.

Shelly Banks beach at the beginning of Irishtown Nature Park.

The north side of it is relatively smoothly built with granite blocks, but on the south side those blocks are supported by irregular blocks to form an artificial cliff. This rocky stretch extends westwards towards Ringsend until it reaches what was formerly called the Green Patch, a kind of island that stayed dry even at normal high tides. This is no longer an island now but it has a small sandy beach.

The little spit of sand at the eastern end of the Poolbeg Peninsula in general is only under water at especially high tides.

The next stretch south of the Great South Wall was used for landfill and eventually formed the Poolbeg Peninsula, with the southernmost part left to nature. Over the years part of this turned into Irishtown Nature Park which borders the sea, forming a green strand with rocks.

Along the sea in Irishtown Nature Park.

'Zebra' boulder beside the sea in Irishtown Nature Park.

It was not all left to nature. Some of the boulders have been turned into artworks.

The rocks provide places for seabirds to nest and forage for food before some of them fly back to their breeding regions further north.

Sometimes it is hard to believe that this bit of nature is at the edge of a metropolitan area with more than a million inhabitants. But then, turning a corner, a reminder of the enthusiasm of this metropolis for rugby and soccer appears in view: the Aviva Stadium.

The path connecting Irishtown Nature Park with Seán Moore Park is a wide and smooth macadamised cycling and pedestrian path like a good, narrow road near a small country town.

Another little sandy cove is situated where the coast turns in a right angle from Seán Moore Park into Sandymount Strand. This is favoured in good weather by families with small children. At low tide it is quite wide, but even at high tide it does not disappear completely.

Seán Moore Park is at the border between Irishtown and Sandymount. On its southern end the monumental *Gallán na Gréine do James Joyce* by Cliodhna Cussen has been erected. The title translates into English as 'A Solar Pillar for James Joyce'. It is arranged so that every year at sunrise on

Aviva Stadium from Irishtown Nature Park.

Modern connection between Seán Moore Park and Irishtown Nature Park.

Cliodhna Cussen, 'Gallán Na Gréine do James Joyce'.

the winter solstice a ray of light appears to align itself along the two elements of the sculpture. It was unveiled in December 1983 by Lord Mayor Michael Keating on behalf of Dublin City Council.

Since the sculpture was erected the park has matured. The sculpture might have worked as a huge sundial in the beginning, but the stones in the grass around the standing stone can just about be discovered. The 'Solar Pillar' itself on the other hand seems to start leaning to one side.

The view from Sandymount Strand towards Dublin Port, especially in the dark, shows much industry and gives no indication that there could be big green patches of nature around.

THE SEA WALL

Nearly from the edge of Seán Moore Park the sea wall has an extension of almost 2km along the coast of Sandymount and part of that of Merrion. It was built more or less at the high water line of an average tide.

This wall is one of the oldest and definitely the longest man-made structures in the area. It was ordered by Richard Fitzwilliam, Seventh Viscount Fitzwilliam of Merrion and Baron Fitzwilliam of Thorncastle, who had it erected in 1791 to protect his land as the digging of clay in the area in 'Lord Merrion's Brickfields' had caused the rather low lying ground in parts to sink below sea level.

At some stage this wall was opened at intervals with steps leading down to the strand. For flood defence reasons these were blocked during recent years.

When not every local dwelling had running water, public water taps were built into the wall. Once the water supply had improved, this was no longer necessary and the water pipes were removed. In the Sandymount part of the sea wall one such place can still be seen because the original protective stone structure around the former tap is still there, though the tap itself has been removed.

Further south the wall is no longer directly at the edge of the sea at full tide. The wall is still beside the road, but on its other side something else has been constructed.

Stretching for approximately 1 kilometre along the Strand Road, the Promenade is a popular walking place and provides outstanding views over Sandymount Strand to Poolbeg, Irishtown Nature Park and Dun Laoghaire. Construction of the Promenade commenced in the late 1960s with final landscape works being completed in the mid 1970s.[1]

The sea wall in Sandymount.

THE PROMENADE

It is highly likely that it was because of the promenade that Sandymount Strand gained a Green Coast Award in 2007 for which a commemorative plaque was erected.

In 2008 Sandymount even entered a Blue Flag pilot phase to obtain Blue Flag status for 2009. For the period of 2010 to 2013, however, the water

The surroundings of a water tap that has been removed.

quality was only regarded as 'sufficient' with the potential of less than sufficient status.[2] The quality of the water had deteriorated so much that Dublin City Council found it wise to put up a warning sign, considering that Irishtown and Sandymount Strands had been places where people collected cockles, advising that people collecting any shellfish for consumption should ring a lo-call number or use the website: http://www.fsai.ie to check any possible risks.

'An Cailín Bán' by Sebastián (Enrique Carbajal González) at the northern end of Sandymount Promenade.

In general the promenade has proved to be very popular, not only by the people of Dublin 4. The three car parks on the promenade are well patronised though they are pay-and-display now to discourage people from leaving their cars in them all day while working locally.

The northern end of the promenade is marked by a large public sculpture:

In November 2002 the City Council erected a sculpture entitled 'An Cailin Ban' by the Mexican artist Sebastián. The sculpture was donated to the City by the Mexican Government and now stands as a significant focal point at the northern end of Sandymount Promenade.[3]

There is actually a prelude to the positioning of this work as the former chairman of the OPW, Brian (Barry) Murphy describes in his memoirs:

The Mexican ambassador offered the OPW (or anyone as it turned out) a large outdoor sculpture by the Mexican artist Sebastián as a gift. He had acquired it in Japan where it was called Geisha. I told him we would accept it in the OPW and suggested that it be renamed An Cailín Bán. The

Green Coast Award (2007) plaque on Sandymount Promenade.

location in mind for it was by the lake in Farmleigh. This did not suit as the ambassador regarded a waterside setting inappropriate, and the gift was withdrawn. He then offered it to Dublin City Council who put it by the strand in Sandymount.[4]

Dublin City Council had intended to position the sculpture further south on the promenade, but after it had been erected there, residents protested that such a modern sculpture would not fit in with the Victorian house fronts on that part of Strand Road, so the work was moved. There still are people who do not like it, and as Dubliners are fond of inventing nicknames for public sculptures (and sometimes buildings) for some this statue is known as 'The Sore on the Shore'.

There were more protests when lamps were installed at the promenade, as some people were afraid that the lamplight during the night would disturb birdlife on the strand. To allay those fears Dublin City Council promised to switch the lamps off at 10 p.m. But the street lights on Strand Road – only a couple of metres beside the lamps on the promenade – remain on all night, without adversely affecting avian life.

Shortly before the promenade and Strand Road cross the border between the townlands of Sandymount and Merrion, an antique pump survives on the land side, just in front of the sea wall, on the footpath of Strand Road. It still has the handle that was pulled to draw water, but it no longer functions. Its spout is in the shape of an animal's head resembling a lion's head with ram's horns.

The best known feature of Sandymount after Sandymount Green and the strand is Sandymount Tower, one of the Martello Towers built along the Irish coast between 1804 and 1806 as a defence against a possible Napoleonic invasion. Sandymount tower is one of four 'double' towers, which meant that from the beginning it carried two 24-pounder cannons on its roof. (The other three double towers are at Dalkey Island, Williamstown and Ireland's Eye.) Double towers have a slightly bigger diameter than the others. Sir Henry James described Sandymount Tower as it was in 1862:

It was 50 feet (15m) in external diameter. The external circular wall was 10 feet (3m) thick, with the internal space being 30 feet (9m) in diameter. It was entered on the land side at first-floor level by an external winding metal stairway 3 feet (0.9m) wide; and machicolation in the parapet above made it possible for the garrison to drop missiles through vertical slots on to the heads of those attempting to force entrance.

The first floor was the living-quarters for the garrison of 12. The floor below, which was reached by a helical stairway 4 foot (1.2m) in diameter and contained within the thickness of the wall, was used as the kitchen and for the master gunner's stores. It contained also the magazine, where 30 barrels of gunpowder could be held. Beneath this floor, which was brick-arched on thick stone walls, there was a water storage tank. The vaulted stone roof, protected by a parapet, was reached by the helical stairs. It supported guns, probably 18- or 24-pounders, which were mounted on a roller system that enabled them to be aimed in any direction over a wide arc. The roof adjacent to the machicolated segment contained a shot furnace that could make cannon-balls red-hot, to be used for setting fire to sails and timber in wooden ships.

Modern excavation shows that the walls were founded on massive grillage of square-section pitch-pine, arranged in three layers.

A small annexe to the tower on the bay side contained an external privy, an ashpit and a coal store, and there was also an internal privy built into the thickness of the circular wall.[5]

This describes the tower when it was in military use. Today an 'external privy' still can be found on the north side of it, albeit quite a modern one which is coin-operated.

The site for the tower had been purchased in May 1806 from Viscount Fitzwilliam supposedly for the sum of £30 5s 0d. Martello towers were the property of the Board of Ordnance and later the War Department. The border of the area the War Department owned was marked by border stones usually showing an arrow. The older ones have the inscription 'B O' for Board of Ordnance, later the inscription was 'W D' for War Department. Some of these could not be put on the actual border. If that was the case they described where the border was. This is the situation at the Sandymount tower where the western border of the site is on Strand Road. The border stone at the foot of the tower has the inscription

W↑D
N⁰ 2
33FT 11IN
WEST

This means that the border is 33ft 11in (10.35m) west of that stone, in other words more or less in the middle of St John's Road where it hits the roundabout on Strand Road. (The mark in the bottom stone of the tower proper, on the left of the border stone, is a bench mark for surveying.) According to the 1907 OS map, border stone W↑D N° 1 was just to the north of the tower and was removed when the promenade was built and W↑D N° 3 was south of the tower in what is now the sunken garden. According to the same map the border between the townlands of Sandymount and Merrion that comes down St John's Road eastwards to the tower just swings round the tower northwards so that Sandymount Tower is actually on Merrion townland.

The tower itself stands empty, though its outside wall of granite blocks has lately been cleaned and re-grouted by a conservation firm.

Sandymount Tower is the only Martello Tower on the eastern coast of Ireland that has as its fundament a 'massive grillage of square-section pitch pine, arranged in three layers'[6] as just at that spot the coast was very sandy and bedrock could not be found. Possibly since the beginning of the twentieth century a house was erected beside the tower, first on the north and later on the south side of it. This at times was occupied by a shop or even a café and restaurant in past years. Old photographs still show it, together with the steps to the original front door on the first floor. On some postcards it looks as if those steps would lead to the top floor of the tram line No. 3 or 4, which had their terminus at the tower.

According to *The Martello Towers of Dublin*[7] the tower's cannons were tested in 1806 and in the same year they engaged in a military exercise that included the Pigeon House Fort and some horse artillery when both cannons fired across Sandymount Strand. This was just an exercise; the cannons were never used against an enemy. The Sandymount and Williamstown towers were disarmed in 1865. After that Sandymount Tower was leased to the Earl of Pembroke. Later it was bought by the Dublin Tramway Company, who broke doors through the walls in the ground floor so that it could be used as a passenger waiting room.

One of those doors must have started its life somewhere else, as it gives 1822 as the year of its making. In that year there were no doors in the ground floor of Martello towers. A photograph used on an old postcard shows that this door and the window above it was not yet in existence at the beginning of the twentieth century.

Another old postcard, slightly younger than the last one according to the design of the tram, shows a little house as an annex to the tower on the north side, but the tower itself still had no doors on the ground floor and no windows on either the north or the south side.

It seems as if the thick walls of the tower were broken through for doors and windows in the first decades of the twentieth century.

The south side of Sandymount Tower.

Later two of the ground floor openings got doors like the one on the south side with the misleading date '1822' and the first floor ones including the original door became windows, as did the ground floor opening facing St John's Road.

In 1945, during the 'Emergency' an anti-aircraft gun and searchlight were installed at the tower. The gun was used only once.[8]

In the 1970s there was a motion that Dublin Corporation should buy the tower to use it as a maritime museum, but the Corporation refused to pay the asking price of £13,000.

At some stage the annex shown on the old postcards was taken down and another building was erected around the seaside half of the tower. This housed a restaurant or café. There still is an annex on this side of the tower, but the former one has been taken down and a new one erected. On the modern photograph it is hidden by a tree. Whatever it was planned for did not emerge, as the building has stood empty for years, though the grounds are swept occasionally, the railing is painted from time to time and in case a flood is threatening, the low-lying garden is protected by sandbags.

There used to be a nice, if tiny, sunken garden on the south side of the tower in front of the annex, but lately that has been defaced by the presence of machinery.

The ground floor door on the south side of Sandymount Tower.

Sandymount Tower seen from the south (Merrion) side. (From an old postcard)

Sandymount Tower, c. 1920. (From Bernard Share, *Time of Civil War: The Conflict on the Irish Railways 1922–23* (Collins Press, Wilton, Cork, 2006))

For many tourists Sandymount Tower is the first attraction they think of when they hear of Sandymount. That is because they mix up Sandymount Tower with Sandycove Tower, which features in James Joyce's *Ulysses*. Sandymount features in *Ulysses* as well, relating to Sandymount Strand, especially the stretch beside the Sandymount Parish Church Star of the Sea.

Further south the remains of the Merrion Baths from 1883 come into view, which have been described in the chapter about Merrion.

There are no natural rocks on the Ringsend to Merrion section of the strand. Rocks were used to fortify the promenade, but certain views of the ruins of Merrion Baths can also suggest the presence of rocks.

No traces can now be found of the earlier Merrion Baths shown in the 1865 map near Merrion Gates.

DANGERS OF SANDYMOUNT STRAND

The way the sand stretches far towards the east at low tide is an invitation to venture out for quite a distance from the sea wall towards the edge of the water, walking or riding a bike, pedalled or motorised. Especially in good weather this invitation is near irresistible. Some years ago it was even possible to access the strand by car. At that time it was said that at least one

Garden beside Sandymount Tower, 2007.

A 'rocky' look-out from Merrion Baths.

car a year on average was lost. This happened when a careless driver, who was not familiar with the conditions on the strand, drove out far and did not look at what happened behind until it was too late. He would find that the car was on a sand island surrounded by water too deep to drive through or else by sand too soft and wet, so that the wheels had no traction. Usually in those cases the driver managed to reach solid land again, leaving the car behind, which in most cases had disappeared by the next low tide. Cars no longer have access to Sandymount and Merrion Strand, but accidents of a similar type happen regularly when people walk too far out, suddenly finding themselves surrounded by water as they have not noticed the water rising with the incoming tide.

The authorities are well aware of the danger and for many years there has been a warning sign opposite some of the steps down from the promenade to the strand which points out the danger. First time visitors to the strand often laugh when they see this sign with the inscription 'Danger! Persons going 200m beyond this notice are in danger of being stranded by incoming tide', especially when they first come to the strand at high tide when this sign is surrounded by water. They do not know how flat this shore is and how far the water will recede at low tide. The exposed sand flats have an area of around 2km^2 and at low tide extend for more than 1.5km (1m) from the shore at their widest point in Sandymount.[9]

Depending on weather conditions nobody will even try to go the distance the sign mentions. In a strong easterly gale it is not only dangerous to walk on the strand, but on the promenade as well. And even driving a car along Strand Road at high tide with a strong easterly wind blowing has its disadvantages as the sea has been known to splash far across the sea wall and even the road.

It really is very pleasant to paddle along on a warm summer day with your bare feet in the flat pools of warm water that are left at low tide. Just remember that the water will be back and usually faster than expected, even when in the beginning the rise seems to be slow, especially on a calm day when the water surface stays calm enough to mirror the industrial structures on the Poolbeg Peninsula.

Every summer brings a couple of reports about people having to be rescued from the strand. Some years ago, for instance, a couple were walking happily along the biggest and firmest of the sandbanks – the one that only disappears when the tide is nearly fully in. This couple definitely were not used to the quick changes of the tides on Sandymount Strand. The very low gradient means that the strand will have a huge extension at low tide and yet completely disappears at high tide. The couple, like the car drivers mentioned

Sandymount Strand at high tide.

before, had not looked behind them for quite some time. When they did, the water had cut them off and what had been a sandy peninsula only a quarter of an hour before was then an island, and the stretch of water between that island and the firm coastline looked quite deep to them. Some people, who had noticed the couple, alerted the lifeboat at Dún Laoghaire. Others who lived on Strand Road had also observed the situation and organised a rescue kayak. They then paddled out to the couple and putting the paddle vertically onto the ground showed them thus, where the water was less deep. The gentleman rolled up his trouser legs and carefully following the path the kayakers showed him, carried his lady into safety. When the lifeboat arrived, they were nearly on land, but most likely they got a lecture about the dangers of the strand.

Another incident occurred on Monday, 3 August 2015, a bank holiday. It was important enough to make the RTÉ News on that day and was not only mentioned on the news websites of RTÉ but also in some newspapers. This incident involved two people and their dogs. A Garda helicopter crew spotted that they were surrounded by water and informed the Irish Coast Guard. The Garda helicopter still managed to land on the sandbank, but could only take one person and one dog on board. Shortly afterwards the coastguard helicopter did not find enough dry land anymore to touch ground and had to airlift the second person and the other dog.

Poolbeg chimneys at low tide.

Walking on the strand can be especially dangerous in fog. Fogs can develop quite suddenly at the coast and not being able to see exactly which direction it is to firm land can be very frightening. In those situations even a lifeboat crew will find it very difficult to detect people in distress.

Another danger, but one that rarely leads to dramatic rescue actions, is to try and walk from Sandymount Strand to the Green Strand at Irishtown

The remains of Merrion Bath floating in grey fog.

The strand in winter.

Nature Park or even the sand of Shelly Banks. A small sandy triangle at the northern end of Sandymount Strand stays dry even at normal high tides. At low tide the stretch in front of this and the coastal path leading east might look nearly dry as well, but it is never firm. The ground there is more silt than sand and anybody trying to walk there will sink deeper and deeper into the slush.

Apart from that there was, some time ago, something that might have turned into a danger, not for people directly, but for the strand itself. Around 2011 people walking along the promenade saw something that worried them a lot. Anxious questions were asked but the answer was reassuring, at least for some. There was to be no drilling for oil, with all the possibilities of pollution of sea and coast. The drilling rig they saw was related to waste water disposal. The possibility of pollution in Dublin Bay by this activity was not discussed. But just a year later the danger seemed to loom even stronger, because at the beginning of 2012 applications had been made for permission for trial drillings for oil east of Dalkey. After many protests the firm that had a prospecting licence decided not to avail of it as they could foresee too many difficulties with both residents and ecologists.

View towards Howth from Sandymount Strand.

Not stranded, just parked out in the bay.

WEATHER AND CLOUDS

Most of the houses on Strand Road opposite the promenade date from the Victorian period and can be very attractive from an aesthetic point of view. Despite this most people on the promenade look in the other direction, over the sea, where the views can be stunning, especially on clear days. At low tide the expanse of sand is vast and it is easy to see how people may be tempted to walk too far out.

Looking south the outlines of Dún Laoghaire and Dalkey can be made out on the horizon. Looking east, Wales is out of the visual range from the promenade (it is possible to see right across the Irish Sea from the hills if the weather is exceptionally clear).

Sometimes it looks as if ships are stranded. When the tide is out it is not always easy to see if something is a strip of water between two sand banks or the beginning of the sea proper. Often ships that arrive earlier than expected are 'parked' in the bay, waiting for the time allotted to them on the quays of Dublin Port to arrive.

Unfortunately it is not always sunny. Misty weather can create quite mysterious views. At times the border between fog-covered sea and misty sky cannot be recognised. At other times, especially on frosty winter days, it is so clear that you can see down to Bray Head, past the southern end of Killiney Bay.

Like elsewhere in Ireland the weather can change from one moment to the next – from sunshine to dark clouds. When both sun and rain occur together another name for Ireland comes to mind: The Isle of Rainbows.

Every year at first light of Easter Sunday the Episcopal, Methodist, Presbyterian and Roman Catholic communities hold an ecumenical service on Merrion Strand. To watch the sun rising during one of these services is unforgettable.

NATURE ON THE STRAND

Nature lovers will find much of interest on the strand and promenade. Seán Moore Park and Irishtown Nature Park give food and shelter to quite a number of passerines: song thrushes and blackbirds, wrens, tits, goldfinches, chaffinches, greenfinches and linnets among them and even the occasional stone chat or rock pipit. Something flying very early in the morning or late in the evening in a fluttering style is, however, most likely not a bird but a bat.

Irishtown Nature Park is interesting as it was not planted by official gardeners like other parks. It was formed by landfill above the sea floor. It was then covered with soil. Some of the land thus reclaimed was used for industry, but another stretch was left to nature in the sense that nobody planted anything. Soon enough plants started to grow from seeds blown in or arriving in bird droppings, developing a green cover over the wasteland, which is a continuing process. For the average visitor the plants here might not be very interesting, but botanists have studied them eagerly to learn about the sequence in which plants move into waste ground. And remember: not every yellow composite flower is a dandelion. If it is low growing it might be coltsfoot (in very early spring) or later one of the hawkweed family, which has taller growing members. It could also be a sow thistle. And there are not only yellow flowers growing in Irishtown Nature Park, nor only composite ones.

It is not only in the Nature Park that nature can be found. Some interesting plants grow in rather unlikely places like at the edge of the promenade in the cracks between tar and rocks.

Greater Sea Spurrey is a very low growing perennial with flowers that are less than 10mm across. It does not seem to appear every year. At the edge of the tarred promenade dandelion and red valerian are common and some sycamore bushes grow there. By cutting these down in winter Dublin City

Council makes sure that the plants stay in a bushy form instead of growing into tall trees.

Just beside it you might find rock samphire which, as its name suggests, is growing quite happily among the rocks.

Rock samphire does not need much soil. It can grow in very narrow spaces, some of them so small that one wonders how and from what the plant gets its nourishment. Some of those places are the cracks between boulders, or even more astonishing, the mortar of walls like on the sea wall near Merrion Gates.

There are other plants that also can grow between the rocky boulders that secure the coastline. All of those plants have to be able to survive not only the salty atmosphere but also the occasional drowning in salt water. The sea aster is one of those plants:

> This is a clever little plant which spends a good part of its life standing with its feet, and sometimes more than its feet, in seawater. Other times it manages to gain a foothold on cliff faces on what appears to be remarkably little soil.[10]

In our modern times people have forgotten that the sea aster is edible as are many other wild plants.

> A superb, tender, salty, succulent plant with a complex sweet flavour with hints of iron and nut. Even large leaves are tender and delicious and remain so after flowering and well into autumn. The flower stalks, flowers, roots and seeds are not worth eating.[11]

From the end of the Promenade the view across the sandy part shows a system of dunes just developing, the fine sand particles kept in place by the root system of marram grass instead of being blown or pulled away by wind and waves.

Further on, at the border between Merrion (Dublin 4) and Booterstown (County Dublin) the catchment area of sand being driven in by the sea on the east of the railway line has led the strand to expand. As this area is watered by some of the many little streams coming down from the Dublin mountains, it is not easy to access, even on foot, which makes it even easier for nature to assert its rights without interference by human beings and their dogs. This wild strand has its own fascination.

The whole of Dublin Bay is a protected area as it is used by a great variety of sea birds and waders as their winter quarters. But even in summer many birds can be observed. Gulls are there all year round. The largest gull in the

Rock Samphire, Merrion end of the promenade with the ruins of Merrion Baths and the Poolbeg Chimneys in the background.

Sea Aster, Sandymount Promenade.

bay area is the Great Black-backed Gull, with an overall length of around 700mm. The slightly more common Herring Gull tends to be 100mm shorter. Its wings are grey on top with just the tips black. Both have yellow beaks with a red dot on it and pink legs.

Another gull is more common than the Herring Gull and can be found far inland as well. This is the Black-headed Gull. The name is confusing as the heads of those gulls are not black, but chocolate-brown and only in winter. During the rest of the year they just have a dusty dark brown smudge behind their eyes. They have black wing-tips, red legs and a thin and rather long red beak.

The Black-headed Gull is considerably smaller than either Great Black-backed or Herring Gull at just under 400mm in length, so it usually is easy to differentiate between them. It can, however, be mixed up with the Mediterranean Gull which is the same size, though adult birds have white wing-tips and a broader red bill with a black ring around it.

The descriptions given here all refer to adult birds; there can be quite a variation in colours, especially for juvenile birds that may have reached adult size already but not yet adult plumage.

Similar to gulls are the terns, which are smaller and slimmer, with a longer and narrower beak and forked tails like swallows. Common terns can be seen all year long on the Great South Wall where they hover over the water before suddenly diving to catch small fish. They usually fish on the Liffey side of the South Wall. From Merrion Strand terns can be watched in the evening when they come down to roost in the sandy stretch between Merrion and Booterstown.

Grey Herons are usually connected with lakes and rivers and even with fields where they hunt mice. But they do also appear on the coast in the Booterstown – Merrion – Sandymount area where they fish in the sea.

Grey Herons are the tallest birds on this strand, reaching up to over 900mm. Their relatives, the Little Egrets, only arrived in Ireland during recent decades from continental coasts where they are especially numerous

A great black-backed gull (foreground) and herring gull (background).

A black-headed gull.

around the Mediterranean. Nowadays they even breed in Ireland. They are less often seen inland, but at the coast they fish like the Grey Heron. Both species can be seen on the artificial island in Booterstown Marsh beside the DART station where sometimes over a dozen Little Egret congregate with a couple of Grey Herons.

Not the tallest, but most likely the heaviest birds that can be seen in winter on the strand from Irishtown to Merrion are Brent Geese, the pale-bellied variety that arrives in autumn and stays until late spring. They grow to around 600mm, which is small for a goose. They usually appear in flocks and can be quite noisy. Pale-bellied Brent Geese breed in Arctic Canada. Nearly the entire Canadian Brent Goose population flies in winter from there to Ireland. Dublin Bay is an important place for them, both north and south of the Liffey. They feed on eel grass, which is rather plentiful at Merrion Gates, but occurs along the whole of Sandymount Strand.[12] This however is not their exclusive food, as they often can be seen on grassy areas all over Dublin (for instance occasionally on the pitches of Monkstown Rugby Club and YMCA Cricket Club) and to see them

Terns coming to roost between Merrion and Booterstown.

A little egret.

flying – and hear them honking – in flocks of 200 and more across the Dublin sky is impressive.

Winter is the best time for birdwatching, as many waders arrive in autumn and leave in spring for their breeding grounds far in the north. Sometimes a few stay over the summer but they would be a lot less obvious, especially as the casual walker on the strand does not expect to find them. It is easiest to watch birds when the tide is half out. Unluckily that is also the time that many dogs are let off their leads and quite often those dogs get to the birds, chasing them away before one has time to identify them.

Turnstones are plentiful in winter, remaining near rocks turning shells and stones at the water's edge to look for small animals underneath. They do that even at times when the tide is nearly in, so that even dogs would not have enough space to run around on the narrow rim of sand the high water leaves uncovered.

Sometimes Turnstones mix with Sanderlings and when seen against the sunlight it can be difficult to decide which is which. Luckily in winter Sanderlings are white with pale grey bellies and wings while Turnstones, though also white underneath, have brown backs with very distinctive

Brent geese on Merrion Strand.

Turnstones in winter plumage.

patterned wings in black, brown and white colours, which look stunning when the birds are seen in flight.

Distinctive and sometimes colourful as those waders look, on part rocky, part sandy beach, they are marked in a way that it can be rather difficult to make them out until they start moving around.

Of similar size as Turnstones and Sanderlings, but just a little bit smaller, are the Dunlins. Turnstones and Sanderlings are winter guests on our coasts whereas Dunlins also breed in Ireland, though not in this area.

It is easy to spot Oystercatchers. With their black and white body and red beak and legs they look quite striking. In flight their wings show a black and white pattern. Their cry ('Peik! Peik!') is quite distinctive as well and easy to distinguish from the calls of other birds on the strand. They are there all year round, but their numbers greatly increase in winter.

Dunlin.

ACTIVITIES

All sorts of activities are possible on a strand. The obvious one is to bring children, food and something to drink, along with a newspaper or book and somebody to mind the toddlers while they are busy digging.

There are many other options, like exercising your dog while having a conversation on your mobile phone. Nothing against dogs, but Sandymount Strand is a protected area for birds, and dogs should always be kept on a lead. The vast majority of dog owners do not stick to this rule and Dublin City Council does not seem to enforce it. Not only birds suffer from this. With all the dogs on the strand it is questionable if you should have small children down there digging up whatever they find (which is not always shells in the sand.)

If the weather is not too cold but with a steady breeze and if the tide is not too far out you can watch kitesurfers the whole length of the strand, from the Shelly Banks at the far end of Irishtown to Merrion Strand.

If there are not too many people around, you occasionally can watch somebody practise golf strikes or hitting a sliotar with a camán, though that does not happen as often as it used to. To actually get involved in such activities the tide has to be out, the wind should not be too strong, it should not rain and as well as that there should be few people on the strand.

Weather conditions can influence all sorts of outdoor activities and on one occasion the people of Sandymount were lucky enough to watch Larry

Having a rest after all that hard digging.

Kitesurfing on Merrion Strand.

Yazzie of the Meskwaki Nation, Iowa, USA give a demonstration of the traditional dance of his country.

Lately access for four-wheeled motor vehicles to the strand officially is no longer possible, so it is not clear how a quad-bike got onto the strand or where it wanted to go. It looks as if the fellow riding it might be heading for the Old Baily Lighthouse, but he definitely will not get there with that type of machine.

There are no stables in or around Sandymount anymore, but horse transporter boxes occasionally appear on Strand Road near the southern end from where it is possible to get onto the strand even on horseback. Down there on the strand then they will collect, wait for the others, discuss the route and set off.

Those who find a saddle too hard to sit on can always sit in a little cart that is pulled by a horse.

All sorts of vehicles will be found on or at least near the strand or the promenade. 'Found' seems to be the word for the lonesome bicycle, though it is more than likely that it is not lost at all and its owner will appear out of the mist just at the moment that somebody or other gets the idea to 'liberate' the poor bike that has been left behind.

Quad bike on Sandymount Strand.

The sand is firm enough for horses and riders.

Trotting along.

'Gone for a walk'.

Merrion Baths with graffiti.

Exercise machines on the promenade.

Endless activities are provided by the Sandymount Baths or at least by what is left of them. They are something special. Some people want to do away with them, because they are an eyesore, some people want to change them so that they are not an eyesore anymore and other people, who do not want any change whatsoever, refuse to accept that they are an eyesore and want them to stay the way they are. In the meantime graffiti artists find them great.

Apart from anything else the remaining walls, especially the one facing the promenade, provide a good shelter against cold easterly winds. A recent report, however, found the remains of the baths were at least in parts unsafe and it has to be decided if they should be repaired or removed.

Lately the promenade has turned into a kind of fitness trail, with many features that some people might recognise from the gym. They are brightly coloured and seem to be well accepted, especially in dry weather and not only by children.

And if all that is too energetic for you, you can of course just sit on one of the many benches and watch the ferries come and go or the yachts from the Dún Laoghaire yacht clubs move silently along the horizon.

SOURCES AND FURTHER READING

Ball, Francis Elrington, *An Historical Sketch of the Pembroke Township* (Dublin: Alex. Thom & Co. Ltd, 1907).

Ball, Francis Elrington and Hamilton, Everard, *The Parish of Taney* (Dublin: Hodges, Figgis, & Co., 1895).

Bennet, Douglas, *Encyclopaedia of Dublin* (Dublin: Gill & Macmillan, 1991).

Blacker, Revd Beaver H., *Brief Sketches of The Parishes of Booterstown and Donnybrook, in the County of Dublin* (Dublin: George Herbert, 1860).

Bolton, Jason, Carey, Tim, Goodbody, Rob, Clabby, Gerry, *The Martello Towers of Dublin* (Dún Laoghaire-Rathdown County Council and Fingal County Council, 2012).

Burke, Helen, *The Royal Hospital Dublin, A Heritage of Caring 1743–1993* (Dublin: The Royal Hospital Donnybrook and The Social Science Research Centre UCD, 1993).

Butler, Revd Richard (ed.), *Registrum Prioratus Omnium Sanctorum juxta Dublin* (Dublin: Irish Archaeological Society, 1845).

Conroy, Colin, *Historic Merrion* (Dublin: Maidenswell Research, 1996).

Corcoran, Michael, *Our Good Health* (Dublin: Dublin City Council, 2005).

Corlett, Christiaan, *Antiquities of old Rathdown. The Archaeology of South County Dublin and North County Wicklow* (Bray, Co. Wicklow, Wordwell Ltd, 1999).

Cowell, John, *Dublin's Famous People and Where They Lived* (Dublin: The O'Brien Press, 1980).

Cromwell, Thomas Kitson, *Excursions through Ireland, Province of Leinster, Vol. II* (London: Longman, Rees, Orme, and Brown, 1820).

D'Alton, John, *The History of the County of Dublin* (Dublin: Hodges and Smith, 1838).

de Bhaldraithe, Tomás (ed.), *English – Irish Dictionary* (Baile Átha Cliath: Oifig an tSoláthair, 1959).

de Courcy, John W., *The Liffey in Dublin.* (Dublin: Gill & Macmillan Ltd, 1996).

Delaney, Ruth, *The Grand Canal of Ireland* (Dublin: The Lilliput Press/ OPW, 1995).

Donnelly, Revd N., *Short Histories of Dublin Parishes, Part I The Sacred Heart, Donnybrook. Star of the Sea, Sandymount. St Mary's, Haddington Road. St Patrick's, Ringsend* (Dublin: Catholic Truth Society of Ireland, 1905).

Dublin's Diving Bell: A History (Dublin: St Andrew's Resource Centre, 2003).

Gandon, James (Jr.), *The Life of James Gandon, Esq., M.R.I.A.,F.R.S, Etc., Architect, With original Notices of Contemporary Artists, and Fragments of Essays.* Prepared for Publication by the Late Thomas J. Mulvany. (Dublin: Hodges and Smith, 1846).

Gaskin, James J., *Varieties of Irish History: from Ancient and Modern Sources and Original Documents.* (Dublin: W.B. Kelly, 1869).

Gilligan, H.A., *A History of The Port of Dublin* (Dublin: Gill & Macmillan Ltd, 1988).

Gogarty, Oliver St John, *As I was going down Sackville Street.*, (London: Sphere Books Ltd, 1968).

History and Description of St Mary's Church, Star of the Sea, Irishtown (Irishtown: Report of the Committee Appointed to Erect the Dean O'Connell Memorial, 1884).

Sandymount Green, Dublin 4. Conservation and Management Plan (Dublin: Howley Hayes Architects, April 2015).

Ireland: Official Industrial Directory Compiled by Department of Industry and Commerce (Dublin: The Stationery Office, 1955).

Joyce, Weston St John, *The Neighbourhood of Dublin* (Dublin: M.H. Gill & Son, Ltd, 1939).

Joyce, James, *Ulysses* (London: The Bodley Head Ltd, 1964).

Kearns Blain, Angeline, *Stealing Sunlight. Growing up in Irishtown* (Dublin: A. & A. Farmar, 2000).

Kennedy, Walter, *Shipping in Dublin Port 1939 –1945* (Durham: The Pentland Press, 1998).

Kiely, Benedict, *Dublin* (Oxford: Small Oxford Books, Oxford University Press, 1983).

Le Fanu, W.R., *Seventy Years of Irish Life, being Anecdotes and Reminiscences* (London: Edward Arnold, 1893).

Lewis, Richard, *The Dublin Guide: or, a Description of the City of Dublin, and the Most Remarkable Places within Fifteen Miles* (Dublin: R. Lewis, 1787).

Lewis, Samuel: *The Topographical Dictionary of Ireland* (London: S. Lewis & Co., 1837).

McKenna, Denis (ed.), *A Social and Natural History of Sandymount* (Dublin: Sandymount Community Service, 1993)

McKenna, Denis (ed.), *The Roads to Sandymount, Irishtown, Ringsend* (Dublin: Sandymount Community Services, 1996)

Murphy, Margaret & Potterton, Michael, *The Dublin Region in the Middle Ages. Settlement, Land-Use and Economy.* (Dublin: Four Courts Press Ltd, 2010).

Murray, K.A.: *Ireland's First Railway* (Dublin: Irish Railway Record Society, 1981).

Ó Maitiú, Séamas: *Dublin's Suburban Towns 1824–1930* (Dublin: Four Courts Press Ltd, 2003).

Prendergast, Elizabeth and Sheridan, Helen, *Jubilee Nurse: Voluntary District Nursing in Ireland, 1890–1974* (Dublin: Wolfhound Press, 2012).

Russell, John, *The Haigs of Bemersyde* (Edinburgh and London: William Blackwood & Sons, 1881).

Saunders, Barry and Bradshaw, David, *Sandymount* (Dublin: Sandymount Association of Youth, 1975).

Shaw, Henry: *The Dublin Pictorial Guide & Directory of 1850* (Belfast: Friar's Bush Press, 1988); reprint of 'Henry Shaw: New City Pictorial Directory 1850 (Dublin: Henry Shaw, 1850).

Smith, Cornelius F., *The Shipping Murphys* (Blackrock Co. Dublin, Albany Press, 2004).

Somerville-Large, Peter, Daly, Mary E., Murphy, Colin: *The Mount Street Club* (Bray, Co. Wicklow: Foxrock Media Ltd, 2014).

Sweeney, Pat, *Liffey Ships and Shipbuilding* (Cork: Mercier Press, 2010).

The Old Township of Pembroke 1863 – 1930 (Dublin: City of Dublin Vocational Education Committee, 1993 and 2011).

Townsend, Brian, *The Lost Distilleries of Ireland* (Glasgow: Neil Wilson Publishing Ltd, 1999).

Walsh, Eamon, '*Sackville Mall: The First One Hundred Years*': *The Gorgeous Mask*, Dublin 1700–1850 (Dublin: Trinity History Workshop, 1987).

Winn, Christopher, *I Never Knew That About Ireland* (London: Ebury Press, 2006).

NOTES

INTRODUCTION

1   Samuel Lewis, *A Topographical Dictionary of Ireland* (London: S. Lewis & Co., 1837).

CHAPTER 1

1   Margaret Murphy & Michael Potterton, *The Dublin Region in the Middle Ages. Settlement, Land-Use and Economy* (Dublin Four Courts Press Ltd, 2010), p. 88.
2   J.W. de Courcy, *The Liffey in Dublin* (Dublin: Gill & Macmillan Ltd, 1996), p. 202.
3   Walter Harris, *The History and Antiquities of the city of Dublin* (Dublin: Laurence Flynn and James Williams, 1766), p. 127.
4   James Joyce, *Ulysses* (London: The Bodley Head Ltd, 1964), p. 56.
5   Oliver St John Gogarty, *As I was going down Sackville Street* (London: Sphere Books Ltd 1968), p. 296.
6   There are several variations of the name de Ridelesford, e.g. de Riddeleford, de Riddlesford or de Riddleford.
7   Registrum Prioratus Omnium Sanctorum juxta Dublin (Dublin: Irish Archaeological Society, 1845), p. 67.
8   Registrum Prioratus Omnium Sanctorum juxta Dublin (Dublin: Irish Archaeological Society, 1845), p. 68.

CHAPTER 2

1   Samuel Lewis, *A Topographical Dictionary of Ireland, Vol. II* (London: S. Lewis & Co., 1837), p. 516.

2   Richard Killeen, *Historical Atlas of Dublin* (Dublin: Gill & Macmillan Ltd, 2009), p.14.

3   J.W. de Courcy, *The Liffey in Dublin* (Dublin: Gill & Macmillan, 1996), p. 325.

4   John D'Alton, *The History of the County of Dublin* (Dublin: Hodges and Smith, 1838), p. 855.

5   Samuel Lewis, *A Topographical Dictionary of Ireland*, Vol. II (London: S. Lewis & Co., 1837), p. 516.

6   Beaver H. Blacker, *Brief Sketches of The Parishes of Booterstown and Donnybrook, in the County of Dublin* (Dublin: George Herbert, 1860), p. 24.

7   *The Old Township of Pembroke 1863–1930* (Dublin: City of Dublin Vocational Education Committee, 1993), p. 19.

8   Beaver H. Blacker, *Brief Sketches of The Parishes of Booterstown and Donnybrook, in the County of Dublin* (Dublin: George Herbert, 1860), p. 54.

9   John D'Alton: *The History of the County of Dublin* (Dublin: Hodges and Smith, 1838), p. 854.

10 http://www.sailcork.com/index.php/blog/full-story/lightships-off-the-irish-coast (accessed April 2016).

11 James J. Gaskin, *Varieties of Irish History: from Ancient and Modern Sources and Original Documents* Appendix F.W.B. Kelly (Dublin 1869), p. 380 f.

12 *A Social and Natural History of Sandymount* (ed. Denis McKenna) (Dublin: Sandymount Community Service, 1993), pp. 22, 24.

13 Michael Corcoran, *Our Good Health* (Dublin: 2005, Dublin City Council), p. 95.

14 Helen Burke, *The Royal Hospital Dublin, A Heritage of Caring 1743–1993* (Dublin: The Royal Hospital Donnybrook and The Social Science Research Centre UCD, 1993), p. 178.

15 www.epa.ie/licences/lic_eDMS/090151b280168c3b.pdf (accessed March 2015).

16 Michael Corcoran, *Our Good Health* (Dublin: Dublin City Council, 2005), p. 112.

17   Richard Lewis, *The Dublin Guide: or, a Description of the City of Dublin, and the Most Remarkable Places within Fifteen Miles* (Dublin: R. Lewis, 1787), p. 139.

18   Richard Lewis, *The Dublin Guide: or, a Description of the City of Dublin, and the Most Remarkable Places within Fifteen Miles* (Dublin: R. Lewis, 1787), p. 230.

19   http://dlharbour.ie/historical/maritime/(accessed March 2015).

20   Samuel Lewis, A Topographical Dictionary of Ireland, Vol. II (London: S. Lewis & Co., 1837), p. 516.

21   Walter Harris, *The History and Antiquities of the City of Dublin, from the Earliest Accounts* (Dublin: Laurence Flynn & James Williams, 1766), p. 264.

22   Margaret Murphy & Michael Potterton, *The Dublin Region in the Middle Ages: Settlement, Land-Use and Economy* (Dublin: Four Courts Press Ltd, 2010), p. 394.

23   *Dublin Weekly Chronicle*, 5 October 1748.

24   John D'Alton, *The History of the County of Dublin* (Dublin: Hodges and Smith, 1838), p. 857.

25   Pat Sweeney, *Liffey Ships and Shipbuilding* (Cork: Mercier Press, 2010), p. 8.

26   Ibid.

27   H.A. Gilligan, *A History of The Port of Dublin* (Dublin: Gill & Macmillan Ltd, 1988), p. 102.

28   Pat Sweeney, *Liffey Ships & Shipbuilding* (Cork: Mercier Press, 2010), p. 11.

29   Ruth Delaney, *The Grand Canal of Ireland* (Dublin: The Lilliput Press/OPW, 1995), p. 178.

30   *NewsFour*, February 2011.

31   Peter Somerville-Large, Mary E. Daly, Colin Murphy, *The Mount Street Club* (Bray, Co. Wicklow: Foxrock Media Ltd, 2014), p. 241 ff.

32   *Ireland: Official Industrial Directory. Compiled by Department of Industry and Commerce* (Dublin: The Stationery Office, 1955), p. 91 and National Archives: Census 1901 and Census 1911.

33   *The Irish Times*, Property Section, 1 December 2011.

34   www.coastguardsofyesteryear.org/articles.php? article_id=245 (accessed March 2016).

35   K.A. Murray, *Ireland's First Railway* (Dublin: Irish Railway Record Society, 1981), p. 50.

36   Barry Saunders and David Bradshaw, *Sandymount* (Dublin: Sandymount Association of Youth, 1975, p. 11.

37   John D'Alton, *The History of the County of Dublin* (Dublin: Hodges and Smith, 1838), p. 849.

38   Barry Saunders and David Bradshaw, *Sandymount* (Dublin: Sandymount Association of Youth, 1975), p. 17.

39   G. Fletcher, 'Industries and Manufacture' in *Leinster East and West, The Provinces of Ireland* ed. George Fletcher (London: Cambridge University Press, 1922), p. 165.

40   Pat Sweeney, *Liffey Ships & Shipbuilding* (Cork: Mercier Press, 2010), p. 144.

41   Smith, Etta Catterson, reporting for 'The Lady of the House' about a morning round in the Dublin South-East District in 1892, as quoted in: Prendergast, Elizabeth and Sheridan, Helen, *Jubilee Nurse. Voluntary District Nursing in Ireland, 1890–1974* (Dublin: Wolfhound Press, 2012), p. 38.

42   Pettigrew & Oulton Street Index 1834 (http://www.swilson.info/po1834.php?pageno=13) (accessed November 2015).

43   Brian Townsend, *The Lost Distilleries of Ireland* (Glasgow: Neil Wilson Publishing Ltd, 1999), p. 146.

44   www.johndore.co.uk (accessed November 2015).

45   http://www.swva.co.uk/lot-46-morgan-44-4-seater-1977 (accessed July 2015).

46   https://www.education.ie/en/Publications/Inspection-Reports-Publications/Whole-School-Evaluation-Reports-List/report1_03917V.htm (accessed November 2016).

47   G. Fletcher, *Industries and Manufacture. In: Leinster East and West, The Provinces of Ireland* (ed. George Fletcher) (London: Cambridge University Press, 1922), p. 148.

48   http://www.ringsendcollege.ie/page.php?id=2title=Second%20Level (accessed November 2016).

49   Revd N. Donnelly, *Short Histories of Dublin Parishes, Part 2 The Sacred Heart, Donnybrook. Star of the Sea, Sandymount. St Mary's, Haddington Road. St Patrick's, Ringsend* (Blackrock, Co. Dublin: Carraig Books, 1977), Originally published (Dublin: Catholic Truth Society of Ireland, 1912). pp. 81, 84.

50   http://www.swilson.info/showcodub1848.php?pageid=ring (accessed July 2015).

51   www.dia.ie/architects/view/3948 (accessed March 2015).

52   http://www.newsfour.ie/2014/02/regal-house-to-re-open/ (accessed March 2015).

53   The *Irish Independant*, 29 November, 1921.

54   *The Irish Times*, 21 December 1943.

55   http://familytreemaker.genealogy.com/users/m/u/r/William-Thomas-Murphy-Leinster/WEBSITE-0001/UHP-0105.html (and equivalent other persons of that family) (accessed February 2015).

56   Cornelius F. Smith, *The Shipping Murphys* (Blackrock Co. Dublin: Albany Press, 2004).

57   John Cowell, *Dublin's Famous People and Where They Lived* (Dublin: The O'Brien Press, 1980), p. 44.

58   Benedict Kiely, *Dublin* (Oxford: Small Oxford Books, Oxford University Press 1983), p. 77.

CHAPTER 3

1   Richard Lewis, *The Dublin Guide: or, a Description of the City of Dublin, and the Most Remarkable Places within Fifteen Miles* (Dublin: R. Lewis, 1787), p. 148.

2   Leinster East and West, *The Provinces of Ireland* (ed. George Fletcher) (London: Cambridge University Press, 1922).

3   J.W. de Courcy, *The Liffey in Dublin* (Dublin: Gill & Macmillan Ltd, 1996) p. 202.

4   Douglas Bennet, *Encyclopaedia of Dublin* (Dublin: Gill & Macmillan, 1991), p. 107.

5   John D'Alton, *The History of the County of Dublin* (Dublin: Hodges and Smith, 1838), p. 851f.

6   Peter Costello, *Dublin Churches* (Dublin: Gill & Macmillan, 1989), p. 124.

7   Revd N. Donnelly, *Short Histories of Dublin Parishes, Part I The Sacred Heart, Donnybrook. Star of the Sea, Sandymount. St Mary's, Haddington Road. St Patrick's, Ringsend*. Originally published 1905. Facsimile edition with an introduction by Dr Thomas Wall (Blackrock County Dublin: Carraig Books, 1977), p. 12.

8   John D'Alton, *The History of the County of Dublin* (Dublin: Hodges and Smith, 1838), p. 857f.

9   http://www.dia.ie/architects/view/2043 FULLER.+JAMES+FRANKLIN (accessed November 2016).

10 Kurt Kullmann, *Rugby Town: The Sporting History of D4* (Dublin: History Press Ireland, 2016), p. 14.

11 Walter Kennedy, *Shipping in Dublin Port 1939–1945* (Durham: The Pentland Press, 1998).

12 Denis McKenna (ed.), *The Roads to Sandymount, Irishtown, Ringsend (Dublin: Sandymount Community Services, 1996)*, p. 70f, as well as additional websites found when searching for those ships' names on the internet.

13 Thomas Kitson Cromwell, *Excursions through Ireland, Province of Leinster, Vol. II*, Longman (London: Rees, Orme, and Brown, 1820), p. 26.

14 Liam McNiffe, *A History of the Garda Síochána* (Dublin: Wolfhound Press, 1999), p. 6.

15 http://archiseek.com/tag/george-l-oconnor/ (accessed November 2016).

16 Reproduced in Denis McKenna (ed.), *A Social and Natural History of Sandymount* (Dublin: Sandymount Community Service, 1993), p. 151.

17 Michael Corcoran, *Our Good Health: A History of Dublin's Water and Drainage* (Dublin: Dublin City Council, 2005), p. 83.

18 Angeline Kearns Blain, *Stealing Sunlight: Growing up in Irishtown* (Dublin: A.&A. Farmar, 2000), pp. 187 ff.

19 http://www.dublincity.it/main-menu-services-culture-sport-and-recreation-sports-and-fitness-centres-leisure-centre-locations-18 (accessed July 2015).

20 http://www.dublincity.ie/sites/default/files/content/RecreationandCulture/SportsFacilities/LeisureCentres/Locations/Documents/2014%20Timetable%20and%20Prices.pdf (accessed July 2015).

21 http://www.avivastadium.ie/getting-here/ (accessed July 2015).

22 http://www.libraryireland.com/irishartists/richard-cranfield.php (accessed October 2016).

23 Francis Elrington Ball, Everard Hamilton, *The Parish of Taney* (Dublin: Hodges, Figgis & Co., 1895), p. 90.

24 Angeline Kearns Blain, *Stealing Sunlight: Growing up in Irishtown* (Dublin: A.&A. Farmar, 2000).

CHAPTER 4

1   Tomás de Bhaldraithe (ed.), *English–Irish Dictionary* (Baile Átha Cliath: Oifig an tSoláthair, 1959). Entry: 'shale'.

2   www.gsi.ie/NR/rdonlyres/EBE7C28D-FAD2-42EA-92BD-8CC2CFA0809F/0/DublinHistoricIndustryDatabaseReport.pdf (accessed May 2015).

3   http://www.dublincity.ie/sites/default/files/content//YourCouncil/Local AreaServices/SouthEastAreaDocuments/FINAL_Sandymount_VDS.pdf (accessed May 2015).

4   http://www.nationalarchives.ie/PDF/PembrokeEstatePapers.pdf (accessed July 2014).

5   www.kennetpans.info/index.php?option=com_content&view=article&id=150&Itemid=354 (accessed May 2015.)

6   John Russell, *The Haigs of Bemersyde* (Edinburgh and London: William Blackwood and Sons, 1881).

7   http://europepmc.org/articles/PMC2197807/pdf/brmedj04665-0048.pdf (accessed January 2017). Many thanks to Robin Hughes in Sheffield for pointing out this rare example of a Victorian apparatus in Sandymount.

8   Richard Lewis, *The Dublin Guide: or, a Description of the City of Dublin, and the Most Remarkable Places within Fifteen Mile*s (Dublin: R. Lewis, 1787), p. 234.

9   Thomas Kitson Cromwell, *Excursions through Ireland, Province of Leinster, Vol. II* (London: Longman, Rees, Orme, and Brown, 1820), p. 27.

10 James Gandon (Jr.), *The Life of James Gandon, Esq., M.R.I.A.,F.R.S, Etc., Architect, With original Notices of Contemporary Artists, and Fragments of Essays. Prepared for Publication by the Late Thomas J. Mulvany* (Dublin: Hodges and Smith, 1846), p. 142 f.

    [The editor Thomas James Mulvany, a painter himself and for some time living in Sandymount, was one of the eleven that William Ashford selected as co-founding members of the Royal Hibernian Academy (RHA).]

11 humphrysfamilytree.com/Humphrys/sandymount.park.html (accessed May 2015).

12 Samuel Lewis, *A Topographical Dictionary of Ireland, Vol. II* (London: S. Lewis & Co., 1837), p. 544.

13   http://www.rds.ie/cat_historic_member_detail.
      jsp?itemID=1101433&item_name=Robert%20Corbett (accessed
      May 2015).

14   Samuel Lewis, *A Topographical Dictionary of Ireland, Vol. II*
      (London: S. Lewis & Co., 1837), p. 544.

15   History and Description of St Mary's Church, Star of the Sea,
      Irishtown. Report of the Committee Appointed to Erect the Dean
      O'Connell Memorial. Irishtown 1884.

16   Denis McKenna (ed.), *The Roads to Sandymount, Irishtown,
      Ringsend* (Dublin: Sandymount Community Services 1996), p. 90.

17   *The Old Township of Pembroke 1863–1930* (Dublin: City of Dublin
      Vocational Education Committee, 1993), p. 21.

18   Denis McKenna (ed.), *A Social and Natural History of Sandymount*
      (Dublin: Sandymount Community Service, 1993), p. 51.

19   Revd N. Donnelly, *Short Histories of Dublin Parishes, Part I The
      Sacred Heart, Donnybrook. Star of the Sea, Sandymount. St Mary's,
      Haddington Road. St Patrick's, Ringsend.* Originally published
      1905. Facsimile edition with an introduction by Dr Thomas Wall.,
      (Blackrock County Dublin: Carraig Books, 1977), p. 52.

20   Ibid. p. 55.

21   History and Description of St Mary's Church, Star of the Sea,
      Irishtown. Report of the Committee Appointed to Erect the Dean
      O'Connell Memorial. Irishtown 1884.

22   http://methodisthistoryireland.org/churches/Christ%20Church,%20
      Dublin.pdf.pdf (accessed December 2015).

23   http://sandymount.weebly.com/ (accessed December 2015).

24   A brief Guide to the Heritage Features of St John's Sandymount
      (Dublin: no year), p. 14.

25   Joe Curtis, *Mount Merrion* (Dublin: The History Press Ireland,
      2012), p. 12.

26   Revd N. Donnelly, *Short Histories of Dublin Parishes, Part I The
      Sacred Heart, Donnybrook. Star of the Sea, Sandymount. St Mary's,
      Haddington Road. St Patrick's, Ringsend.* Originally published
      1905. Facsimile edition with an introduction by Dr Thomas Wall
      (Blackrock County Dublin: Carrig Books, 1977), p. 29.

27   Ibid.

28   Donal S. Blake, cfc, *Mary Aikenhead (1787–1858), Servant of the
      Poor* (Sandymount, Dublin, RSC Caritas (without year), p. 93.

29 www.irishsikhcouncil.com/GurdwaraDublin.htm (accessed October 2012).

30 http://churchrecords.irishgenealogy.ie/churchrecords/ details/707c720520887 (accessed November 2016).

31 http://newsarch.rootsweb.com/th/read/IRL-WICKLOW/2003-03/1047980488 (accessed November 2016).

32 Ireland. Official Industrial Directory. Compiled by Department of Industry and Commerce. (Dublin: The Stationery Office, 1955).

33 Séamas Ó Maitiú, *Dublin's Suburban Towns 1824–1930* (Dublin: Four Courts Press Ltd, 2003), p. 147.

34 W.R. Le Fanu, *Seventy Years of Irish Life, being Anecdotes and Reminiscences* (London: Edward Arnold, 1893), p. 163.

35 Ibid., p. 203.

36 Beaver H. Blacker, *Brief Sketches of The Parishes of Booterstown and Donnybrook, in the County of Dublin* (Dublin: George Herbert 1860), p. 94.

37 www.national archives.ie/PDF/PembrokeEstatePapers.pdf (accessed October 2015).

38 John D'Alton, *The History of the County of Dublin* (Dublin: Hodges and Smith, 1838), p. 859.

39 homepage.eircom.net/~sandymountsch/our_school/our_school%201. htm (accessed October 2016).

40 http://www.abigailrieley.com/a-sentence-of-death/ (accessed September 2015).

41 http://www.thepeerage.com/p33858.htm#i338576 (accessed July 2015).

42 http://www.oxforddnb.com/view/article/52698 (accessed November 2015) and John Crawford, *Around the Churches: The Stories of the Churches in the St Patrick's Cathedral Group of Parishes* (Dublin: Select Vestry of the St Patrick's Cathedral Group of Parishes, 1988), p. 65.

CHAPTER 5

1   Revd N. Donnelly, *Short Histories of Dublin Parishes, Part III Booterstown, Blackrock, Stillorgan, Kilmacud and Dundrum*. Originally published 1905. Facsimile edition with an introduction by Dr. Thomas Wall. (Blackrock County Dublin: Carraig Books, 1977), p. 85.

2   Margaret Murphy & Michael Potterton, *The Dublin Region in the Middle Ages. Settlement, Land-Use and Economy* (Dublin: Four Courts Press Ltd, 2010), p. 266.

3   Foclóir Gaedhilge agus Béarla, *Being the Thesaurus of the Words, Phrases and Idioms of the Modern Irish Language*. Compiled and edited by Revd Patrick S. Dinneen. New edition, revised and greatly enlarged, published for the Irish Text Society (Dublin: Educational Company Ltd, 1927), Entry: 'muirbhthean'.

4   Barry Saunders and David Bradshaw, *Sandymount* (Dublin: Sandymount Association of Youth, 1975), p. 1.

5   Francis Elrington Ball, *An Historical Sketch of the Pembroke Township* (Dublin: Alex. Thom & Co., Ltd, 1907), p. 28.

6   James J. Gaskin, *Varieties of Irish History: from Ancient and Modern Sources and Original Documents* (Dublin: W.B. Kelly, 1869), p. 188.

7   Colin Conroy, *Historic Merrion* (Dublin: Maidenswell Research, 1996), p. 4.

8   Richard Lewis, *The Dublin Guide: or, a Description of the City of Dublin, and the Most Remarkable Places within Fifteen Miles* (Dublin: R. Lewis, 1787), p. 198.

9   Blacker, Revd Beaver H., *Brief Sketches of The Parishes of Booterstown and Donnybrook, in the County of Dublin* (Dublin: George Herbert, 1860), p. 52.

10 Samuel Lewis, A Topographical Dictionary of Ireland, Vol. II (London: S. Lewis & Co., 1837), p. 366.

11 Colin Conroy, *Historic Merrion* (Dublin: Maidenswell Research, 1996), p. 3.

12 Blacker, Revd Beaver H., *Brief Sketches of The Parishes of Booterstown and Donnybrook, in the County of Dublin* (Dublin, George Herbert, 1860), p. 20.

13 Colin Conroy, *Historic Merrion* (Dublin: Maidenswell Research, 1996), p. 14.

14   Weston St John Joyce, *The Neighbourhood of Dublin* (Dublin: M.H.
      Gill & Son, Ltd, 1939), (first published 1912), p. 29.

15   Samuel Lewis, A Topographical Dictionary of Ireland, Vol. II
      (London: S. Lewis & Co., 1837), p. 366.

16   Henry Shaw, *New City Pictorial Directory 1850* (Dublin: Henry
      Shaw 1850), (p after Grafton street).

17   Colin Conroy, *Historic Merrion* (Dublin: Maidenswell Research,
      1996), p. 9.

18   http://www.dublincity.ie/sites/default/files/content/
      RecreationandCulture/DublinCityParks/NewsEvents/Documents/
      Merrion%20Baths%20Sandymount%20Strand_%20Draft%20
      Report.pdf (accessed December 2015).

19   Peter Somerville-Large, Mary E. Daly, Colin Murphy, *The Mount
      Street Club* (Bray, Co. Wicklow: Foxrock Media Ltd, 2014), p. 149.

20   Colin Conroy, *Historic Merrion* (Dublin: Maidenswell Research,
      1996), p. 16.

21   http://www.dia.ie/works/view/36945/building/CO.+DUBLIN,+DU
      BLIN,+MERRION+ROAD,+NO.+294+%28IMCO%29 (accessed
      March 2015).

CHAPTER 6

1   http://www.dublincity.ie/main-menu-services-recreation-culture-
     dublin-city-parks-visit-park/sandymount-strand (accessed August
     2015).

2   https://www.epa.ie/pubs/reports/water/bathing/bathing_water_
     report_2013.pdf (accessed August 2015).

3   https://www.google.ie/search?q=sebastian:+an+cailean+ban&ie=utf-
     8&oe=utf-8&gws_rd=cr&ei=dU2yVcecBLSR7AaUr6KgAg (accessed
     July 2015).

4   Brian (Barry) Murphy, *Public Work* (2014), p. 91. Quoted with the
     permission of Brian (Barry) Murphy.

5   Sir Henry James: Plans of the Barracks etc. in the County of Dublin,
     being part of the Dublin or Northern District Zincographed in the
     Topographical Department of the War Offices, 1862.

6   J.W. De Courcy, *The Liffey in Dublin* (Dublin: Gill & Macmillan,
     1996), p. 248.

7   Jason Bolton, Tim Carey, Rob Goodbody, Gerry Clabby, *The Martello Towers of Dublin* (Dún Laoghaire-Rathdowne County Council and Fingal County Council, 2012), p. 145.

8   https://irishmartellotowers.wordpress.com/locations-south-dublin/ (accessed August 2015).

9   http://www.dublincity.ie/sites/default/files/content/ RecreationandCulture/DublinCityParks/Documents/Mgt of Beaches in St Dublin Bay 2006 (accessed August 2015).

10   http://www.wildflowersofireland.net/plant_detail.php?id_ flower=15&wildflower=Aster,%20Sea (accessed December 2015).

11   http://www.gallowaywildfoods.com/?page_id=1633 (accessed December 2015).

12   http://www.dublincity.ie/sites/default/files/content/ RecreationandCulture/DublinCityParks/Documents/Mgt of Beaches in St Dublin Bay 2006 (accessed August 2015).